D1302070

Straddling the Fence

The Danger of Compromise

Anita Whitaker

Publishing Designs, Inc.
Huntsville, Alabama

Publishing Designs, Inc.
P. O. Box 3241
Huntsville, Alabama 35810

All Bible references are from the New King James Version
unless otherwise noted.

Printed in the United States of America

ISBN 0-929540-32-8

With love to my nieces—

Emily
Megan
and
Elana

Contents

Thanks

With deep love and gratitude to my parents, Willard and Janie Whitaker, for teaching me all I needed to know to live a Christian life.

To my grandparents, Roy and Mamie Craig and Pearl Davis Whitaker, though no longer with us, for their examples of "how to live it," which continues to influence me even today.

To my sisters, Barbara Carter and Cheryl Couch, for always being there for me.

To the Lincoln congregation girls' class teachers (Fall quarter 2000): Robbie Cantrell, Dawn Ellenburg, Carla Huggins, Karen Stough, Kelly Swafford, Dawn Wacaster, and Bonnie Williams for your support, your ideas, and your examples. To all the young ladies in that class, thanks for just being yourselves.

To those who read the manuscript or provided valuable comments and suggestions, thank you: Charles Barker, Jean Barker, Robbie Cantrell, Kim Davis, Mike Dozier, Kim Dozier, Byron Laird, Dawn Mercer, Tom Wacaster, Jr., Dawn Wacaster, Bonnie Williams, and Ron Williams.

To Paula Ealy for providing a listening ear while I wrote this book.

To James Andrews and Peggy Coulter for gently and patiently leading me through the publication process.

To Byron Laird ("Dr. B.") for his enthusiasm, knowledge, and wisdom, which are constant sources of inspiration to me.

Special thanks to Ron Williams for his encouragement. Without it, this book would have been neither started nor completed.

Introduction

Whoever hears these sayings of Mine, and does them, I will liken him to a wise man who built his house on the rock: and the rain descended, the floods came, and the winds blew and beat on that house, and it did not fall, for it was founded on the rock (Matthew 7:24-25).

No one can serve two masters; for either he will hate the one and love the other, or else he will be loyal to the one and despise the other. You cannot serve God and mammon (Matthew 6:24).

Who Owns the Fence?

A story is told of a large field with a fence running down the middle of it. On one side of the fence stood Jesus, and on the other side stood Satan. Standing between them, near the fence, was a large group of people.

Both Jesus and Satan began calling to the people in the group, and one by one, each having made up his or her mind, went to either Jesus or Satan. This continued for some time, with Jesus and Satan pleading with members from the group to join them. Soon, Jesus had gathered around Him a group of people from the large crowd, as had Satan.

But one young lady joined neither group. Instead, she climbed upon the fence and just sat there, straddling the fence.

Eventually, Jesus and His followers left and disappeared. Satan began to gather his people to leave also. The young woman straddling the fence watched as Satan began to walk along the fence, looking for something he appeared to have lost.

She asked, "Have you lost something?"

Satan looked straight at her and replied, "No, there you are. Come with me."

"But," said the woman, "I chose neither you nor Him. I'm straddling the fence."

"That's okay," said Satan. "I own the fence."

Why Me?

Are you a fence straddler? I'll admit I have been—even as an adult, but it wasn't always that way. As a teenager, I was known for my unwavering stance on biblical principles.

Growing up in the late '60s and early '70s in a medium-size Southern city, I attended church services faithfully, and there was no question as to where my family and I would be on Sunday morning, Sunday night, and Wednesday night. I was taught the basics of Christianity and morality at an early age by some of the best teachers. I knew my Bible. Yet, somewhere along the way, I lost my direction and traveled way off course for several years.

I blame compromise for those lost years and for my fence straddling. This seemingly harmless trait is often thought of as a virtue, enabling us to settle or avoid arguments by not hurting anyone's feelings. While there is a time and place for mutual consensus on matters of opinion, there is also a time when a Christian must take a stand for what is right.

As with any Christian—given enough time, compromise damaged my Christianity. It weakened my faith, attacking the principles I believed in to the point I could no longer stand up and face times of trouble. Compromise was subtle, clever, and dangerous; it left me with a faith as weak as water, while I settled for a life of complacency and mediocrity.

Why This Book?

The idea for writing this book evolved from my intense desire to "say something" after observing both the younger and older Christian women whose lives crossed my path. Many of the young women were energetic, ambitious, and intelligent; the older Christian women were godly, genuinely concerned for others, and stalwarts in the church. I saw so many good characteristics in all of them, but I was troubled, because I also saw fence straddling, compromise on controversial issues, and uncertainty on basic biblical principles.

I wondered if the older Christian women had taught the younger ones all that they needed to know (Titus 2:3-5). Did any of us understand the consequences of not standing firm for our beliefs? Had the older women merely assumed the younger women knew what they should from the Bible about how to fight sin today? Maybe we only hoped they did. Perhaps the younger women just pretended to know these things; maybe they really didn't.

As an author, I have no real credentials; neither am I a wife, mother, or counselor. To some people, I am just an ordinary person—a quiet career woman, a sister, daughter, and friend; to others, I'm an outgoing and fun-loving extrovert. At times, I wondered if I fit society's image of a Christian woman.

I don't bake pies, I can't sew, I'm not much of a public speaker, and I'm not that good with babies, although I do love them. I play golf, ride motorcycles, and fish; I live on a mini-farm, and I work hard physically. I'm not known for my patience, I'm not the best cook in the world; I'd rather wear tennis shoes than heels, and mow the grass than change a diaper. Perhaps, I'm still a bit rough around the edges. But all those things aside, one fact remained— I am indeed a Christian, and I did have something to say! Thus, this book was begun.

Why These Topics?

The topics presented in this book are certainly not new; neither are the Bible solutions. I don't hear them discussed with the young women in church today, though—issues such as premarital sex, abortion, homosexuality, career problems, greed, materialism, feminism, divorce, remarriage, and others.

I must admit that I, like many of my generation, have been close to some of the issues presented in this book, either by participation or active support. I don't say that with any pride, but to emphasize the reality of Satan living in our world. He is alive and well today, attracting young Christian women just as surely as he attracts the rest of the world.

While my own life has been diverse and sprinkled with many fond memories and experiences, it has lacked fulfillment because I compromised my Christian beliefs: I straddled the fence. Hopefully, a young lady can benefit from studying these issues by looking at some of the unfortunate choices others have made and by examining what the Bible teaches.

The Authority of God

Volumes have been written about every subject presented in this book, so naturally I won't be breaking any new ground. My purpose in addressing them at all is to show the relevancy of the Bible in dealing with today's problems facing young women, and to initiate thought and further study by concerned women. If our young women sit on the seat of compromise, what happens to the next generation? Who will fulfill the mission of the church?

The foundation of this book is the Word of God, and I make no apology for quoting it often. Neither your opinion nor mine really counts for much when you get right down to it. This is the truth that finally brought me back to Christ and His church. I think it's the lesson we all have to learn in understanding anything about this life or the one to come.

Even though problems are indeed plentiful today, it's still a wonderful time to be a young woman. Opportunities abound, potential is unlimited, and success is imminent for those young women willing to "go for it." I hope in some way these lessons and examples are useful to young Christian women who are searching for answers. It is with love and deep humility that I share these thoughts with you.

Anita Whitaker
September 2002

CHAPTER ONE

Let's Party!

Compromising Our Influence

Fence-Straddling Position: "I can do as the world does—just as long as I don't get caught. It's okay to drink and party a little. I'm not such a bad person. Besides, I can handle it!"

Bible Position: "Let us walk properly, as in the day, not in revelry and drunkenness, not in lewdness and lust, not in strife and envy. But put on the Lord Jesus Christ, and make no provision for the flesh, to fulfill its lusts" (Romans 13:13–14).

Scripture Search

Proverbs 20:1   1 Corinthians 6:9–11
Proverbs 23:29–35   Galatians 5:19-21
Proverbs 31:4–7   Ephesians 5:18
Romans 13:13–14   1 Peter 2:11
1 Peter 4:3–5

Say What?

Influence—The power of producing an effect. The way we affect others; sway.

Abstinence—Habitually refraining from drinking alcoholic beverages or taking drugs.

Addiction—Devoted to or surrounding oneself to something habit-forming and physically and/or psychologically destructive.

A "Drink"—Twelve ounces of beer or wine cooler; four ounces of wine; or 1.25 ounces of liquor or whiskey.

Binge Drinking—Consuming five or more drinks in an hour. Drinking to get drunk.

Blood-Alcohol Content (BAC)—A measure of intoxication; varies according to the amount of alcohol consumed as well as weight, sex, and other physical factors.

Sober—Not drunk. Self-controlled and serious-minded.

Gateway Drug—A drug whose use increases the likelihood that a person will go on to try harder drugs.

Club Drugs and Date-Rape Drugs—Illegal drugs that increase sexual desire or are given to another to lower sexual inhibitions.

Revelry—Excessive and boisterous merrymaking, noisy festivity and dancing.

Tolerance—The ability to resist the effects of alcohol and drugs.

Debauchery—Excessive indulgence in sensual pleasures.

Beth breathed a sigh of relief as she closed her locker and walked away for the summer. Her senior year loomed ahead. How exciting! It was good to be alive, young, and free as a bird.

"Beth! Wait up—I want to ask you something."

It was Katie, her best friend. "Spend the night at my house

Friday. I've got something special planned and want you to go along with me."

"Yes?" Beth responded with cautious optimism.

"Oh Beth, Matt invited me and anyone else I know to the rave Friday night over off Highway 71."

"A rave?" Beth asked naively.

"Silly girl!" Katie laughed. " It's just a big all-night party, lots of dancing, the best music ever, great DJs, good looking guys—"

"You will have to count me out," Beth said flatly, considering her Christian reputation. "You know I don't—"

"Oh, this is really just a big end-of-school get-together—you'll meet lots of new people. You don't have to drink if you don't want to. It's no biggie—you'll love it!"

"How are you going to stay out all night without your parents knowing?" Beth was bending a little.

"I've taken care of everything. My parents think I'll be at your house and your parents think you'll be at my house." Katie pushed: "Matt said he would pick us up around ten o'clock at Tom's Quick Mart."

Katie's offer set off a big fight in Beth's brain. I should not do this . . . Maybe I need some new excitement . . . What if Mother finds out? . . . Oh, well, these are my friends . . . Nothing bad is going to happen . . . But it is wrong, isn't it? . . . Aren't you tired of being a Goody-Two-Shoes, Beth?

"Sounds like fun," Beth relented. "I'll go."

"Wonderful, Beth! You won't be sorry!"

The rave was in full swing when they arrived. Beth had never felt so much energy in one place. The techno music was beating a loud and steady pulsating beat, and the place was literally packed. As the midnight hour approached, Beth was totally energized by the music and dancing.

"Hey Beth!" Matt screamed at her above the noise. "I've got something for you. Just try it. Talk about dancing—this pill will kick you really good!"

Beth eyed the pill momentarily. "Sorry, Matt, you know I'm not into drugs."

"Oh, this isn't really a drug—just an Ecstasy tablet. Basically harmless. Makes you want to dance and dance and dance! It's great! I do it all the time. Katie's already taken one tonight."

Beth extended her hand for the pill.

Well, okay, what's the harm, really? *she thought*. Katie looks well enough.

No sooner had she taken the drug than she heard a noise and saw a commotion. "Okay, everyone, the party's over!" the police officer shouted gruffly. "Line up, give me your names and addresses and we're going to the station. We've been watching this place for weeks—illegal drugs everywhere."

Wait! *thought Beth*. I'm not like these other people! I haven't done anything wrong. What's my mother going to say? Why did I do this?

The officer stared demandingly into her face: "Your name, address, and phone number!"

Out the window Beth saw another officer putting Matt and Katie into the police car. Then an officer grabbed her arm and jerked her toward the door. Her mind raced. This can't be happening to me. This can't be happening to me. This can't be—

But it was!

From Ecstasy to pot to pills, illegal drugs are as popular today as during the drug-infested culture of the '60s. Although club drugs, such as MDMA—better known as Ecstasy—are fairly new on the party scene, their popularity has become epidemic among today's youth.

Ecstasy is a popular, illegal stimulant used primarily by young people for energy while partying and dancing. The drug takes effect within 20 to 40 minutes and its effects last from three to six hours, depending on the dosage. Ecstasy is also called the "hug drug," since it produces a feeling of well-being and an increased desire for sex.

Although Ecstasy is touted as a safe and fun party drug, evidence is mounting against it. Recent studies show it is not harmless; it can have a long-lasting negative effect on the brain, altering memory function and motor skills.

Taking Ecstasy causes some users to permanently damage their teeth because they grind them so severely. Some suck on pacifiers or lollipops to keep from gritting their teeth. Other side effects of Ecstasy include increased blood pressure, heart rate, and body temperature, hallucinations, chills, sweating, vomiting, restlessness, depression, hemorrhaging, brain damage, and death. Deaths are usually the result of heatstroke from dancing for long periods of time in hot nightclubs without replenishing lost body fluids.

Date-Rape Drugs

Date-rape drugs, such as Roofies, Special K, and GHB cause muscle relaxation and amnesia. Men sometimes mix a date-rape drug in a soda or an alcoholic drink, and give it to their dates to incapacitate and prevent them from resisting sexual assault.

Rohypnol (Roofies) is a strong sedative similar to Valium but ten times more potent. Roofies are produced and sold legally by prescription in Europe and Latin America; however, the drug is neither manufactured nor approved for medical use in the United States. Roofies cause decreased blood pressure, memory impairment, and muscle relaxation. They slow motor skills and cause deep sleep and amnesia. The drug has no taste or odor, so the victims don't realize what is happening to them until it is too late.

The U.S. Drug Enforcement Administration (DEA) states that two common misperceptions about Rohypnol may explain its popularity among young people. First, many wrongly believe that the tablet is "unadulterated" (safe), because it comes in pre-sealed bubble packs. Second, many mistakenly think its use cannot be detected by urinalysis.

Ketamine (Special K) is a powerful hallucinogen and a legal, prescription drug used by veterinarians as an animal tranquilizer; however, its use by humans is illegal and possession can result in long prison terms. In powder form, Special K is usually snorted but is sometimes sprinkled on tobacco or marijuana and smoked. In liquid form, Special K is mixed with a drink. Either form of Special K causes profound hallucinations, visual distortions, temporary memory loss, nausea, loss of motor control, and potentially fatal respiratory problems.

GHB (Liquid X) is prescribed for narcolepsy and alcoholism. It is also used by some body builders who wrongly believe that it helps them to lose weight. An odorless liquid and slightly salty to the taste, GHB is sold in small bottles. To disguise its taste, it is often slipped into drinks.

The effects of GHB can be felt within 5 to 20 minutes after ingestion and the high can last up to four hours. GHB causes slowed heart rate, respiratory failure, violence or aggression, seizure-like activity, and sometimes coma. A capful of GHB can have the same effect on some people as five beers. Reaction varies with the individual. While one capful might not affect one person, it might kill another. Some former GHB addicts say withdrawal from this drug is so painful they want to kill themselves; the drug has caused many suicides.

Young women, be especially aware of the dangers of club drugs and date-rape drugs. Use your common sense when in a crowd or on a date. Never leave a drink unattended; and never, never accept a drink from a stranger.

Other Drugs

In addition to club drugs and date-rape drugs, many so-called recreational drugs—marijuana, cocaine, PCP, LSD, and heroin—are also readily available today.

Marijuana is most often the drug choice of young women when they begin experimenting with drugs. There is a false notion that pot is not so bad, and that it's only a soft drug used for relaxing and coping with the daily pressures of life. How wrong is that idea!

Marijuana is a harmful drug, especially since its potency has increased more than 275 percent over the last decade. In addition to the physical damage pot inflicts on the lungs and body, the most dangerous element of marijuana is that it takes away a person's motivation, especially harmful in the formative teenage and young adult years.

The Bible does not specifically say, "Do not use drugs," but it does list *witchcraft* as a work of the flesh (Galatians 5:20) and tells us that "they who practice such things will not inherit the kingdom of God."

Witchcraft! you may say. *We're talking about drugs, not witchcraft.*

Yes, *witchcraft,* as it originally appeared in Galatians 5:20, is spelled p-h-a-r-m-a-k-e-i-a. Do you see *pharmacy* there? The first definition of *pharmakeia* is "the use or the administering of drugs."

Just the Facts, Please

In spite of the stir and stigma of illegal drug use, the truth is that the legal drug, alcohol, remains the number one drug problem among young people. Statistics show that first use of alcohol usually begins around age 13, and in 1998, there were over 10 million drinkers in the United States under the age of 21. Although the legal age to buy alcohol is 21, nearly 75 percent of those polled in one survey said they buy their own fairly easily, regardless of their age. Another recent survey also showed that up to 87 percent of high school seniors have used alcohol.

Junior and senior high school students drink 35 percent of all wine coolers sold in the United States. They also consume 1.1 billion cans of beer annually, and college students drink over 4 billion. The Bureau for At-Risk Youth organization reports that more than 60 percent of all homicides, 50 percent of all traffic fatalities, 65 percent of drowning deaths, 80 percent of deaths by fire, 60 percent of child abuse, and 55 percent of arrests are related to alcohol use.

Alcohol kills 6.5 times more youth than all other drugs combined. The three leading causes of death for 15- to 24-year-olds are automobile crashes, homicides, and suicides, of which alcohol is a leading factor in all.

In 1998, Mothers Against Drunk Driving (MADD) reported that nearly 16,000 people were killed in alcohol-related crashes, an average of about one every 33 minutes. Over one million were injured that same year in alcohol-related wrecks. In the United States, 2,750 youths under the age of 21 lose their lives each year in alcohol-related crashes, and 93,000 youths are arrested each year for driving under the influence (DUI).

DUI is a serious offense. A blood-alcohol content (BAC) level of .08 is legal intoxication in most states today, and it doesn't take much alcohol, especially for a small woman, to reach that level. A first-time DUI conviction can result in a suspended driver's license, large fines, increased insurance rates, and even jail time.

From 1982 to 1999, nearly 350,000 persons lost their lives in alcohol-related traffic crashes. More Americans have died in alcohol-related traffic crashes than in all the wars the United States has been involved in since our country was founded! The statistics go on and on.

Why Drink Anyway?

With all this negativity and gloom portrayed, why would anyone start drinking anyway? Why would a person continue to drink? Let's look at six commonly cited reasons below:

1. *"Everyone Else Drinks!"* Young people have always been tempted to drink alcoholic beverages, and today's society is no different. Many young women do not even enjoy the taste of alcohol, but drink it anyway just to be accepted by their friends. A recent MADD study among college students showed some young people are re-thinking that position. Nearly one-third of them said they wished alcohol were not available for campus activities, and nearly 90 percent wished drugs would disappear altogether from their campuses. It's okay not to drink and party!

2. *"You Only Live Once!"* While growing up, some young people experiment with alcohol and other drugs to see what it's all about. Some are neither attracted to it nor tempted by it again. However, others find the attraction strong, and a pattern is established that carries over into adulthood.

   Alcohol is the leading gateway drug. Sixty percent of all drug abusers report that alcohol was the first drug they used. Also, those who use alcohol are six times more likely to use other drugs than those who don't. Experimenting with alcohol and other drugs can eventually lead to addiction, though in the beginning it is difficult to believe this could happen.

3. *"Girls Just Wanna Have Fun!"* Many young women believe that alcohol gives them an edge in talking to others and makes them a bit more sophisticated. While some feel this is true of drinking one drink, it usually never stops there. If a little is good, then a little more will probably make things even better —or so goes the thinking many times. But as drinking increases, so does risky behavior, including sexual activity, in which most people would never get involved if they were sober.

4. *"It Simply Makes Me Feel Good!"* Although a drink might make a person feel "up" initially, this feeling quickly turns downward, since alcohol is actually a poisonous depressant that affects our decision-making, coordination, and ability to drive. Low levels of alcohol in the bloodstream increase the electri-

cal activity in the brain and produce pleasure and euphoria. This is the "buzz" so many people seek, but it is temporary.

Any pleasant effects of alcohol are short-lived, and after drinking more than a couple of drinks, alcohol interferes with the chemical messages in the brain. The after-effects are unpleasant: clumsiness, poor coordination, slurring of speech, staggering, and intoxication.

5. *"It's the Weekend!"* Sometimes, any reason is good enough to celebrate—there's a party, a ballgame, a wedding, or maybe it's just the weekend. "Just because" drinking can lead to the deadly practice of binge drinking, which has become epidemic in high schools and on college campuses. Binge drinkers have only one objective in mind—to get drunk!

Years ago, binge drinking was associated mainly with college fraternities and considered to be a "guy thing," but today statistics show that the number of heavy-drinking young women is significant. Binge drinking can easily kill a person. Since alcohol is a poison, once it enters into a drinker's system and reaches a certain level, the body can no longer withstand what is being put into it. Binge drinkers drink past the point of intoxication, and continue to drink until passing out. While sleeping it off, they often throw up and sometimes die by choking on their vomit.

6. *"I Need To Drink!"* No one plans on becoming an alcoholic. Once addicted to alcohol, the old saying "I can take it or leave it" suddenly becomes a lie, because an alcoholic cannot just take it or leave it anymore. The alcoholic's body craves alcohol and will not be satisfied until getting another drink.

A person can be an alcoholic at any age. One sign of problem drinking or alcoholism is a high tolerance for alcohol, with the drinker being able to drink more and more and handle it without showing signs of drunkenness. This tolerance causes an alcoholic to crave more alcohol just to reach the same level of intoxication reached previously, when drinking only a small amount.

What Does the Bible Say?

Numerous passages in the Bible deal with drunkenness and revelry. Although there's not a verse that specifically says, "Thou shall not drink a beer," plenty of scriptures warn of the devastating effects of excess drinking and drunkenness. The inspired writers of the Bible didn't straddle any fences when dealing with the subject of drunkenness. Proverbs 23:29–32 is an excellent passage that paints a vivid picture of a drinker and presents some wise counsel for abstaining from drinking. Solomon said,

> Who has woe? Who has sorrow? Who has contentions? Who has complaints? Who has wounds without cause? Who has redness of eyes? Those who linger long at the wine, those who go in search of mixed wine. Do not look on the wine when it is red, when it sparkles in the cup, when it swirls around smoothly. At the last, it bites like a serpent, and stings like a viper.

In Romans 13:13–14, Paul encouraged the Christians to live as people belonging to the day and to avoid having wild parties or getting drunk. Galatians 5:19–21 lists drunkenness as a work of the flesh, with those guilty of such not inheriting the kingdom of God. In 1 Peter 4:3, Peter explained how some people had lived before becoming Christians. He said,

> For we have spent enough of our past lifetime in doing the will of the Gentiles—when we walked in lewdness, lusts, drunkenness, revelries, drinking parties, and abominable idolatries.

First Corinthians 6:9–10 also includes drunkenness as one of the sins that can keep a person from entering the kingdom of God, listed alongside adultery, fornication, and murder. It's obvious from these scriptures alone that God does not take drunkenness lightly.

Five Good Reasons Young Christian Women Should Not Drink

Is God trying to limit our freedom and our fun by condemning the use of alcohol? No, He has at least five reasons for commanding us to abstain.

1. *Drinking Destroys Our Christian Influence.* In the *Sermon on the Mount,* Jesus told His disciples they were to be the light of the world and the salt of the earth (Matthew 5:13–16). How can Christians be salt and light if we are just like the world? We are to be peculiar people as Christians—not weird peculiar, but definitely different, since we are God's purchased possession. We are told in Romans 14:21 not to do anything that would cause someone to stumble. Since partying and drinking

are usually of a public nature, our influence as Christian women is greatly diminished if we participate in those activities.

Amy found out firsthand how damaging it was to her Christian reputation to attend parties and participate in questionable activities. A high school friend she hadn't seen in many years approached her one night at one such party. She was shocked to see Amy, beer in hand, since she knew Amy claimed to be a Christian.

"What in the world are you doing here?"—she just blurted it out.

Amy was stunned; she made no response.

Her friend began to reminisce: "Do you remember when we used to play softball together?"

Still silent, Amy nodded knowingly.

Her friend slowly turned and walked away uttering these stinging words: "I thought the world of you back then—you used to be my hero."

Although Amy haughtily dismissed her that night as a drunk, those words still ring in her ears even today. Any influence she had on her friend was totally lost in that one instance by her unwillingness to get off the fence and take a stand. Amy had to admit she was no different from the world, and Christian young women are supposed to be different! We are God's special people. We must take a stand for something, or we'll fall for anything. Peter said it well in 1 Peter 2:9:

> But you *are* a chosen generation, a royal priesthood, a holy nation, His own special people, that you may proclaim the praises of Him who called you out of darkness into His marvelous light.

2. *Drinking Destroys Our Bodies.* Our bodies are referred to as the temple of God (2 Corinthians 6:16). As such, we should be careful how we treat them. Romans 12:1 teaches that Christians are to present their bodies as living sacrifices to God, pure and holy. Alcohol can literally destroy our bodies. The damage is not seen immediately, but the body will eventually break down from excessive drinking.

Overindulging in alcohol is harmful to everyone, but special problems are well documented for female drinkers. The Alcohol Advisory Council states that because women have a higher proportion of body fat and less water in our bodies, alcohol affects us differently and more adversely than it affects men.

Even if a woman is the same size as a man, she will generally feel the effects longer. A woman who weighs the same as a man and drinks the same amount of alcohol will end up with a blood-alcohol content a third higher than the man's.

A woman is more sensitive to alcohol. She will develop alcoholic liver disease within a shorter period of heavy drinking and at a lower level of drinking than a man will. More alcoholic women die of cirrhosis than do alcoholic men, and many women die younger than men with similar drinking patterns.

I've seen seemingly innocent partying destroy the lives of some of my close friends. I remember a young girl with whom I played ball during our high school years who was an outstanding athlete and the fastest girl I had ever seen on a basketball court. She could have easily played on many college teams as a point guard, but Mandy didn't go to college after graduating from high school.

The last time I saw her, she was wasted on drugs and alcohol. Just a few years later, I read of her death in the paper. That brief obituary told nothing of the beautiful girl I remembered. From friends, I learned she had died from cirrhosis after years of heavy drinking. Mandy was only 38 years old when she died.

3. *Drinking Can Damage or Kill Our Unborn Children.* Fetal Alcohol Syndrome (FAS) is one of the leading causes of birth defects and developmental disabilities in the United States and is the leading single cause of mental retardation in the Western Hemisphere. FAS is caused by pregnant women drinking alcohol. Common features of FAS include growth deficiencies; facial defects such as a small head, small eyes, and a pug nose; and central nervous system defects including attention problems, seizures, and learning disabilities. Research shows there is no known safe level of alcohol consumption during pregnancy.

4. *Drinking Destroys Our Self-Image.* Excessive drinking is not cool, vomiting in public is disgusting, and passing out is not a pretty picture. Nothing can destroy our self-image more than constant partying and drinking. The behavioral ill effects

brought on by drinking alcohol can linger for weeks, months, or even years. Not remembering what might have happened at a party the night before, who was there, or what was said to others is embarrassing, demoralizing, and a sure way to lose all self-respect and our credibility to others as a Christian.

5. *Drinking Destroys Our Families, Our Names, and Our Reputations.* Alcoholism is one of the leading causes of depression, violence, and divorce. Families are torn apart when there is an alcoholic in the home. Jobs are lost because of the ill effects of drinking, and money that could be used to support the family is wasted on alcohol. DUI and alcohol-related wrecks become reality. More importantly, reputations and names are destroyed, and Christian influence is lost forever when a person becomes enslaved to alcohol. Solomon said it well in Proverbs 22:1: "A good name is to be chosen rather than great riches." Alcohol, whether used by a mother, daddy, or child, is sure to bring tragedy to a family!

It's Up to You

Alcohol and drug use and addiction will make your life less than it could be. Engaging in these devastating practices will assure you of heartbreak, health issues, and finally spiritual demise. As Christian women, we should embrace all who need help, guidance, and love in their attempts to win over addiction. It's often a hard battle.

If you or someone you love is a user or abuser of any kind of drug, take the time to study the facts concerning addiction, read God's Word for yourself, talk to a trusted friend, and make an intelligent and Christ-centered decision concerning alcohol and drug use. What would Jesus want you to do?

It's Your Turn!

1. How does God expect His children to deal with alcohol?

2. What do you think about the concept of designated drivers?

3. What are the dangers of social drinking?

4. Cite a verse in the Bible that condemns drinking. Also cite a verse that condemns drunkenness and one that condemns drug use.

5. Why are teenagers drawn to alcohol and drugs when they are fully aware of the dangers?

6. What is the number one reason young people drink?

7. How important are companions when it comes to partying?

8. What are some special problems for female drinkers?

9. List some ways in which a young woman can be on guard against date-rape drugs.

10. Is alcoholism a disease or a sin, or both? Explain.

CHAPTER TWO

Everyone Else Is Doing It

Compromising Our Morality

Fence-Straddling Position: "I'm gonna see just how close I can come to sinning, without going over the edge. You only live once."

Bible Position: "Flee also youthful lusts; but pursue righteousness, faith, love, peace with those who call on the Lord out of a pure heart" (2 Timothy 2:22).

Scripture Search

Psalms 119:1–3	Galatians 5:19–21
Psalms 119:9–16	Philippians 4:8
Proverbs 1:10	1 Timothy 1:9–10
Romans 12:1–2	1 Timothy 2:9–10
1 Corinthians 6:9–10	1 Timothy 4:11–12
1 Corinthians 6:18–20	2 Timothy 2:22

1 Peter 2:11

Say What?

Morality—Upright, honest, virtuous, high standards. Rules and standards of conduct and practices. Virtue in sexual matters.

Promiscuous—Frequent and indiscriminate changes in one's sexual partners.

Immodest—Indecent; shameless, forward.

Pornography—Material such as books, photographs, videos, movies, and the Internet that depicts erotic behavior and is intended to cause sexual excitement.

Contraceptives—Devices or drugs that prevent pregnancies (condoms, birth-control pills, etc.)

Lust—Sexual desire or appetite, especially when uncontrolled or illicit.

Abstinence—Refraining from various indulgences, such as sexual relations. Self-restraint.

Chaste—Pure in lifestyle; not having engaged in unlawful sexual relations.

"Safe Sex"—Using condoms during sexual relations to prevent pregnancy or contracting a sexually transmitted disease (STD).

Fornication—Sexual immorality.

"R-r-ring!!" Amanda had been waiting for Cliff's call all week. She raced to catch the phone before the machine picked up.

"Are you busy Saturday night? I thought we'd go see a movie if you'd like." Cliff had asked the right question.

"Sure," she said, straining to hide her excitement. "That sounds good to me."

"I could pick you up around 7:30; the movie starts at 8:00."

"Okay—what's playing?" Amanda asked.

"I thought we could check out the one showing at Westside Theatre. It won all the awards recently—even picked up the best

picture of the year. Everyone I know has already seen it."

"Oh, that one." Amanda hesitated. "I've read all the reviews, and I would really like to see it—but I'm not sure I should."

"Why not?" Cliff asked impatiently. He had spent the past few months trying to break down her Christian values.

"Well, it's rated 'R.' I just don't know—"

"Amanda, can't you just ease up every once in a while? You're sixteen years old! How long will you be tied to your mother's apron strings?"

"Well," Amanda was almost apologetic, "I can't even get into the theatre anyway without an ID."

"Are you kidding? They never check ID's. I've gotten into R-rated movies plenty of times. Trust me, it won't be a problem."

"Well, okay, I guess it'll be all right just this once. It probably isn't all that bad anyway, since it won all those awards."

"You're a smart young lady," Cliff purred. "See you Saturday night at 7:30."

Sitting in the dark theatre, though, Amanda knew she had made the wrong decision. Nudity, explicit sexual acts, cursing, homosexuality, incest—and Cliff sitting beside her.

This movie is really vulgar, *Amanda thought. She mentally kicked herself. Watching Cliff out of the corner of her eye, she knew he was not all she wanted him to be. But even worse, she disliked herself, almost a reflection of Cliff—and she claimed Christ as her Lord!*

She breathed a prayer: One day I won't back down, one day I'll stand up for what's right, one day . . .

Then she reminded herself: "One day" is not on the calendar!

The old-fashioned statement "everyone else is doing it" has been around for many years, and every generation of parents has heard it. Every generation of young people has used it, and the expression continues to apply to many activities today. From vulgar movies and music to smoking, drinking, cursing, immodesty, and premarital sex, it appears today that everyone else is truly "doing it."

Although today's young women seem to be faced with new and different temptations, things haven't changed that much over the years. What has changed is that questionable activities are now more open and that we as Christians have become desensitized to the "in your face" type sin that is constantly shoved down our throats. Consider a few of the following activities and some suggestions for avoiding the consequences of each.

- *Movies—PG, PG-13, R, NC-17, X.* What's the limit for movies? The movie Cliff and Amanda viewed was R-rated, so maybe they should have expected what they got. We must be careful in choosing the movies we see, because even PG and PG-13 films are no guarantee of a movie's quality.

  Movie Morality Ministries discovered that nearly 25 percent of all PG and PG-13 films include coarse, vulgar curse words; about 60 percent take the name of the Lord in vain; 50 percent imply sexual relations, with 30 percent featuring explicit nudity; and about 75 percent display moderate or severe violence and alcohol or other drug abuse. That's just the PG and PG-13 movies; of course, the R- and X-rated movies are even more explicit.

  Christian young people are knowledgeable of these facts and should be choosing better. Sadly, though, one survey of conservative Christian teens narrowed down the types of movies that they had seen over a six-month period: 30 percent reported viewing a G-rated film; 71 percent PG-rated; 76 percent PG-13; 68 percent R-rated; and 10 percent X-rated. We must take a stand against the immorality and violence that is constantly put before us in movies.

- *Television.* Is the TV on in your house? In most of our homes it is. Many people turn on the TV regardless of what's showing. One study reported teenagers between the ages of 12 and 17 watch an average of 22 hours of TV per week. After sleep and time spent in school, children and teenagers spend more time watching TV than any other out-of-school activity.

  By the time the average American child graduates from high school, he or she will have watched about 23,000 hours of television, as compared to the 11,000 hours spent in the classroom. It's not just teenagers, either. Three-quarters of college students have their own televisions in their dorm rooms, half of them have a VCR, and half have cable. The average American adult watches from 27 to 42 hours of TV a week.

TV is not inherently bad, since it provides educational, informative, and constructive programs, as well as entertaining ones. But many people in our society have had enough. They're making the move to just turn off the TV. The negative effects of TV can be seen every day in the violence projected and in the unlimited sexual situations shown, many involving casual sex between unmarried people.

Homosexuality is projected as normal behavior on TV today, and the family is often portrayed as a joke, with many anti-family theme shows being aired. God is usually not mentioned at all by the media, and if He is, His name is usually preceded or followed by a curse word. As Christians, we need to get off the fence and take a firm stand as to what we will allow ourselves to view.

- *Immodesty.* With fashions changing constantly from year to year, how can a young Christian woman dress modestly, yet attractively and fashionably? The tragedy of today's fashion scene is that many young girls are indeed getting the attention they want fashion-wise—but in all the wrong ways. A columnist wrote of a recent trip to the mall.

> They were 12- or 13-years-old and would have seemed so cute, so funny, so girlishly charming, except that they were dressed like hookers. Both wore "barely there" halter-tops, low-cut jeans revealing belly buttons and three inches of tender flesh below that, and high-heeled spikes. They were made up like Madonna on a bad day, lips smeared with raspberry red, eyes outlined raccoon-style. They looked for all the world like two children playing dress-up, only no mothers were coming forward to say it was time to wipe off the makeup, take off the heels, and dress like children again.

Does it sound familiar?

Webster defines modesty as "freedom from conceit or vanity; propriety in dress, speech, or conduct; unpretentious." Expanded, this means modest dress not only covers enough of the body to avoid inciting lust in an observer, but also includes not calling undue attention to ourselves, even though thoroughly covered.

For example, a silk, gold sequined, long-sleeved, floor length, collar-to-the-chin dress would not be modest at a worship service—nor at a football game for that matter—because it is inappropriate costume for the occasion and would draw concentrated interest at these events. Modesty also extends to our jewelry, makeup, and every aspect of our countenance. Are nose rings, tattoos, pierced tongues, and purple hair merely fads or do they draw attention to ourselves in a negative way?

Modesty, to a degree, is also relevant to the times. Unless we're on stage in a character role, Shakespearean dress or the robes and togas of biblical eras are no longer modest because we would be the center of attention should we wear them today. Paul addressed modesty in 1 Timothy 2:9–10 when he said

> that the women adorn themselves in modest apparel, with propriety and moderation, not with braided hair or gold or pearls or costly clothing, but, which is proper for women professing godliness, with good works.

Since males are much more visually stimulated than females, Christian women must be extra careful in their choice of clothing. If there is any doubt about whether an article of clothing is too tight, too short, or too low-cut, then it probably is. A change of clothes might be in order. A police officer or an athlete's uniform intentionally projects a certain image. Do our clothes, jewelry, makeup, and general appearance reflect a Christian image?

- *Premarital Sex.* In his book, *The Christian Woman's Search for Self-Esteem,* Peter Blitchington told the story of Lisa and Jeff, two college freshmen who had been dating for a few months:

> Lisa said, "I'll never forget my first sexual experience. I was under much pressure because I'd never 'done it.' Jeff seemed a nice enough guy—he didn't grab me on the first date or anything. When he asked me to spend Sunday afternoon in his dorm room, I knew what he expected and I decided why not? No man seems to care about virginity today anyway." She continued, "We sat on his bed and kissed, then we lay on his bed . . . and made love." Tears filled her eyes. "Then he leaned over and flipped on the TV. It was so casual to him—so nothing. I felt like he'd wiped his feet on me."

Such stories are not unusual. Many young women say, "I was wrong . . . I feel guilty . . . I feel used . . . I wish I'd waited" when it comes to casual, premarital sex or even sex in a "committed" relationship.

One survey reports that among the nation's ninth graders, 40 percent have had sex; by the tenth grade, 48 percent, and by the eleventh grade, 57 percent. By the time they are seniors, 72 percent of America's teens have had sexual relations. Other studies show that the average age for first-time sexual relations is 15 for girls and 14 for boys.

For the great majority of teens, premarital sex has become a normal and accepted part of growing up. But aren't Christian young people different? Surveys also show about 43 percent of 18-year-olds who come from decent Christian homes, where they have been taught that premarital sex is wrong, are also "doing it."

From the innocent Beatles' song, *I Wanna Hold Your Hand,* to Tina Turner's cynical, *What's Love Got to do with It?* today's generation is no longer primarily concerned with the morality of premarital sex. Many consider premarital sex a rite of passage from childhood to adulthood, and many use it as a way of receiving love regardless of how shallow it may be. Recent surveys show that about 60 percent of the general population and nearly 80 percent of all 18- to 29-year-olds believe that there is nothing wrong with having sex before marriage.

In light of those attitudes, why should a Christian young woman wait for sexual intimacy, and how can she avoid the pitfalls and temptations to "do it" when it seems as though everyone else truly is?

Walt Mueller, in his book *Understanding Today's Youth Culture,* gives five good reasons to wait until marriage.

1. *Physical Reasons.* Although exact numbers are hard to pinpoint, it is estimated that one in five teenagers will contract a sexually transmitted disease (STD). STDs are running rampant and infect 12 million people every year in the United States. Among the most common of about 20 prevalent STDs are gonorrhea, syphilis, genital warts, herpes, and AIDS. These diseases cause infertility, pain, and even death.

   It has been said when a person has sex with someone, he or she is actually having sex with everyone who ever slept with that individual! Women are more vulnerable to catching an STD than are men, and infections are more easily passed from men to women than from women to men.

   Prevention Magazine reports that a woman is eight times more likely to get HIV—the virus that causes AIDS—from a man who is infected than a man is to get HIV from an infected woman. This is after having unprotected sex just once! Abstaining from premarital sex is the only sure way to avoid contracting these diseases.

Another physical reason for abstaining from premarital sex is, of course, the possibility of becoming pregnant. One million American teenage girls (one in ten under age 20) become pregnant each year.

2. *Emotional Reasons.* If we listen to the advice of the world today, all we need to do to make our life more pleasant and secure is to use condoms. Supposedly, condoms will protect us from STDs, keep us from becoming pregnant, and allow us to have sexual freedom. Condoms aren't foolproof, though, and some reports say they are likely to break or fail 10 to 20 percent of the time.

The biggest problem with condoms is not that they might break, but that they can't protect young women against the emotional and traumatic effects of premarital sex. Condoms only attempt to mask the physical aspect of sex; they don't fit over a person's soul. Sex is never just physical, and it always involves more than just the body. Having sexual relations outside of marriage brings an enormous amount of guilt and unrest to those who participate.

3. *Relational Reasons.* Once a young woman crosses the line and gives in to a sexual relationship with her boyfriend, the fun dates are probably over. Strong relationships often end when premarital sex begins, even though the couples may continue to date and spend time together. Sex merely becomes the "main course" and many relationships quickly fall apart after the novelty of having sex with a new partner wears off.

4. *Future Reasons.* Physical limits must be set before getting into a situation where a decision must be made concerning whether or not to have sexual relations. There is the ever-present danger of unwanted pregnancy once premarital sex begins. If a young lady does become pregnant, tremendous decisions that can affect the rest of her life will have to be made concerning her own well-being, as well as that of the father and the unborn child.

When 16-year-old Andrea became pregnant, she was determined to make a go of it. Zach, her 17-year-old boyfriend, had other plans and felt it would not be wise for them to marry at such a young age. While Andrea agreed in principle about their young ages, she began to panic over what to do. Should she keep the baby? What would her parents say? What would her friends at church and school think? Should she try to force Zach to marry her? What would they do for money? Neither she nor Zach had a job and neither had finished high school.

After her pregnancy was revealed, Andrea found herself withdrawing from others, and some of her old friends were suddenly not around anymore. She had to quit high school. She recalled, "Zach broke the news to me that he was going away to college in the fall and that he would try to help out the best he could, but he had to get on with his life."

Andrea was devastated, but she was fortunate to have a caring and supportive family who provided emotional and financial help to her during her pregnancy and the birth of her little daughter. Although she loved her baby dearly and felt she had made the right decision to keep her, Andrea realized the road ahead would be rocky as she began her seventeenth year with a new baby, no husband, no high school diploma, no job, and little money.

Young unmarried women who become pregnant often do suffer many hardships. It's tough for a teenager to have the responsibility of a baby. Most girls drop out of school, and only one-third of teenage mothers receive a high school diploma. In most cases, the teenage father of the child abandons the young woman, and if they do marry, often it doesn't last. Many young unmarried women are left in poverty, delegated to working low-paying jobs, resulting in low self-esteem and depression. Nearly 80 percent of unmarried teen mothers end up on welfare.

5. *Spiritual Reasons.* Premarital sex contributes to various spiritual problems. Many of those who are involved in premarital sex say they feel extreme guilt, shame, low self-esteem, and emptiness. Some feel ostracized from God and the church. Even though a large percentage of young people are indeed "doing it" sexually, one survey reported an overwhelming 98 percent of sexually active teens regretted early sexual involvement.

As much as some try to discount it, premarital sex is sinful. In fact, premarital sex is just another word for fornication. First Corinthians 6:9–10 and Galatians 5:19–21 tell us that those who are guilty of fornication will not inherit the kingdom of God. There's really no way around it—God condemns fornication over and over throughout His Word.

Why All the Rules about Sex?

When I was growing up, parents and kids didn't talk about sex very much. Although the sexual revolution of the '60s changed society's views on sexuality to an extent, one-on-one discussion of it was still uncomfortable. Many parents used the simple explanation then that their children should not have sexual relations because they might get pregnant, get someone pregnant, or contract an STD.

Those reasons might seem irrelevant today, with contraceptives such as the pill and condoms readily available, and drugs such as penicillin available to treat STDs. Jay Kesler gives some excellent advice as to the real reasons why young people should abstain from premarital sexual relations, and those reasons are primarily spiritual ones:

> Young people need to fully understand the spiritual implications of giving themselves to another person sexually—to really have an idea of what it means when two people become one (Genesis 2:24). Once a person takes part in certain intimacies, they can never go back to where they were before. Sex is much too important a part of life to be reduced to just satisfying the sexual appetite or to be used as a game.

God intended that sexual relations be reserved for marriage. Even if a couple is in love and will be married anyway, God condemns sexual relations outside of marriage.

How to Avoid Succumbing to Sexual Temptation

Sex is natural and good within the confines of marriage, as God planned it. In 2 Timothy 2:22, the apostle Paul encouraged Timothy, a young man, to flee youthful lusts. To do that today, consider the following suggestions as ways in which a young Christian woman can avoid sexual temptations:

- *Develop a List of "Do's and Don'ts" concerning Physical Limitations before Dating Starts.* Don't wait to think about this until already in the heat of the moment, since good decisions cannot be made then. Most of the time, the woman has to set the limits and draw the line when it comes to determining how far is too far, sexually speaking.

- *Avoid Places or Occasions Where It Would Be Easy to Yield to Temptation.* Although they may appear innocent, dances, parked cars, dorm rooms, and home alone all offer opportunities for sexual intimacy. In fact, most sexual activity between teenagers takes place in their own homes.

- *Stay Away from Pornography.* Pornography use is often assumed to be a man's issue, but the truth is that pornography is abused by and addictive to both women and men. Accessing pornography through the Internet is now as easy as the click of the mouse, so it's no wonder the pornography business is booming and has skyrocketed to an 8-to-10-billion-dollar-a-year enterprise!

  Since pornography is used privately, it is sometimes referred to as the "secret sin." Viewing or reading pornography is progressive, and what is initially exciting and sexually stimulating to someone will no longer satisfy after a while. Many studies confirm that pornography promotes violence, abuse, and rape, causes extreme guilt and shame, and destroys relationships and marriages. It is always harmful to men and women and always degrading to women.

  Though some people see no big problem with pornography, Christian women should literally run from it. A Christian woman should never accept its use by her boyfriend or husband, and never be lured into participating. Proverbs 4:23 reminds us: "Keep your heart with all diligence, for out of it spring the issues of life."

  It is important what we allow our minds to think about. Philippians 4:8 says we should think on those things that are good, worthy of praise, true, honest, right, beautiful, and pure. Does this sound like pornography? Run. Run! Run!!

- *Respect God's Commandments concerning Fornication.* A healthy respect for what the Bible teaches concerning marriage and sexual relations is important in understanding God's plan for man and woman. People sometimes try to justify premarital or extramarital relationships because it "feels so right," and their particular situation appears to be different from other people's situations. Their relationship is special, it's the real thing, and it could not possibly be wrong—in their own eyes.

Several years ago, this type thinking was referred to as situation ethics. Situation ethics is based on the belief that there is no absolute right or wrong in any matter, but each situation or decision is based on individual circumstances and feelings. But no matter how it might feel, time and again in the Bible, God condemns fornication.

Already Sexually Active?

Although many older Christian women today don't want to accept that their young Christian daughters, granddaughters, and others are sexually active, the facts show differently. Although studies show that young women who have been raised in the church are less likely to have premarital sex, that doesn't mean all refrain.

For any young woman who may already be sexually active, though you may be practicing "safe sex" and have taken all precautions to prevent contracting an STD or becoming pregnant, please reconsider your decision. God knows about the activity, even if no one else does. From a study of the Bible, we've seen that fornication is sinful and displeasing to God.

To be initially forgiven of any sin, one must believe in Jesus as the Son of God, repent of sin, confess Christ, and be baptized to have past sins washed away. When Christians sin, they must repent of the sin, confess it to God and to those offended, and pray to God to forgive it. God stands willing to forgive even if you are already engaging in premarital sex. Regardless of past or present sexual activity, God can and does forgive those who turn to Him, genuinely repent, and stop the sexual activity.

Already Pregnant?

There is also the possibility that a young woman reading this chapter may already be pregnant and not married. You may be frightened and confused, but please do not panic over the situation. If the pregnancy is already common knowledge, trust in the Lord to supply you the courage to deal with your situation in the way He would have you to, and make a good decision concerning your pregnancy. Many who have chosen abortion will tell you that it was the worst decision of their life.

If you are pregnant out of wedlock, consider these suggestions:

- If you are not a Christian, repent and have your sins washed away in baptism.
- If you are a Christian, ask your Christian friends for prayers of forgiveness.
- Don't consider abortion.
- Enlist help from parents, grandparents, friends, and relatives.
- Make a good decision about marrying. Weigh all your options and seriously consider your future before blindly marrying the father of the child. Don't compound one mistake by making another.
- Finish your education.
- Keep yourself and your unborn baby physically healthy.
- Don't forget your family, your friends, or the church.
- Lean on God to supply you with strength and courage.
- Quit beating yourself up. With God's help, do the best you possibly can in your situation.

Don't Get Too Close!

Being human, it is sometimes tempting for us to bend the rules of morality and sexuality a bit by experimenting or taking part in questionable activities. Sometimes we get too close to the edge and sin reaches out and stings. The following story illustrates that quite well.

> An Indian girl climbed high into the mountains where it was freezing cold. Stopping to rest, she noticed a rattlesnake at her feet. The poor, cold snake pleaded with the young girl to take it down to the valley where it was warmer. The girl, listening to the enticing of the serpent, gave in to its pleading. She gathered the snake up into her arms, covered it with her blouse, carried it down the mountain and then gently laid it on a warm rock in the grass. Moments later, the vicious snake raised its head and struck the girl with its poisonous fangs. The girl cursed the snake for striking her as an answer to her kindness, but the rattlesnake only replied, "You knew what I was when you picked me up."

Always remember the message of the snake.

It's Your Turn!

1. How can a young woman dress modestly, yet fashionably? How should a Christian feel about getting a tattoo, wearing a nose ring, or having a pierced tongue?

2. How can you decide what movies are acceptable? Discuss the reliability of the rating method.

3. Why are sexually transmitted diseases (STDs) so hard to talk about? How much at risk do those in your peer group feel themselves to be? How much at risk do you think they are?

4. What does the Bible say about premarital or extramarital sex?

5. Do you agree with the statement "everyone else is doing it" concerning sex? Why or why not?

6. What is situation ethics? Discuss some things that can be right or wrong, depending on the circumstances. Discuss some things that are always wrong.

7. List some problems a young Christian woman faces if she becomes pregnant before marrying.

8. What are some options if a young woman becomes pregnant before marrying?

9. What are some common-sense reasons to save sex for marriage?

10. Why is it dangerous for a married couple to view pornographic movies?

CHAPTER THREE

Abortion:

Pro-Life Woman—Pro-Choice Woman?

Compromising Our Integrity

Fence-Straddling Position: "A woman can do as she chooses with her body. After all, it's her body and it's her right."

Bible Position: "For You formed my inward parts; You covered me in my mother's womb. I will praise You, for I am fearfully and wonderfully made; marvelous are Your works, and that my soul knows very well. My frame was not hidden from You, when I was made in secret, and skillfully wrought in the lowest part of the earth" (Psalms 139:13–15).

Scripture Search

Genesis 1:26–27	Psalms 127:3
Isaiah 49:1	Psalms 139:13–16
Jeremiah 1:5	Proverbs 6:16–19
Psalms 22:9–10	Luke 1:44

Say What?

Integrity—Holding fast to moral and ethical principles; soundness of moral character.

Abortion—To prematurely terminate a pregnancy.

Pro-Life—Opposed to legalized abortion.

Pro-Choice—Favoring legalized abortion.

Fetus—The unborn young of an animal or person.

Viable—A fetus sufficiently developed so as to be capable of living outside the womb.

Roe v. Wade—The 1973 Supreme Court decision that gave American women the right to choose legalized abortion to end unwanted pregnancies.

Trimester—A term or period of three months. Term used to describe the three stages of pregnancy.

Partial-Birth Abortion—A controversial abortion procedure used after four-and-one-half months of pregnancy to six months or even later.

Abortionist—A doctor who performs abortions.

Dr. Edwards looked up from his notes as parents-to-be Jana and Jim took their seats in his office. Without even as much as a greeting he addressed the issue: "Many fetuses like yours will die within a few months after birth, and if it did happen to live longer, there is a strong possibility it may never walk or talk or have a normal life. I recommend you terminate the pregnancy as soon as possible, while the fetus is still in the tissue stage."

Jana didn't remember much after that. Jim was ashen as they left the doctor's office with a list of phone numbers of doctors who could perform the abortion quietly and quickly.

Now, as Jana's hand shook, she called her mother to tell her the news. "Mom, what am I going to do? I never, ever thought I would be in this position. Why is this happening to us? We're Christians and have never even considered abortion before! I just don't know what to do—this is the hardest decision I've ever had to make!"

Mrs. Carter, though alarmed, listened patiently and tried to offer words of consolation.

"But Mom, maybe the doctor has a point—it's only a tissue-like fetus now. Maybe I should have the abortion."

At those words, a long-forgotten scripture from the Old Testament came rushing to Mrs. Carter's mind: "And the Lord said to Moses, 'Who has made man's mouth? Or who makes him dumb or deaf, or seeing or blind? Is it not I, the Lord?'" (Exodus 4:11).

"Jana," she said as gently as she could, "I can only tell you one thing, and then you must make up your own mind. If your decision is as gut wrenching and agonizing as you say—and I have no doubt that it is—that must mean you feel the fetus is truly more than just a blob of tissue. Let's take some time to pray about this and think this through."

Imagine for just a moment that you are extremely hungry— so hungry that no matter what you eat or how much you eat, the hunger remains. My niece Elana is always hungry, and the hunger will never leave her as long as she lives.

She was born with Prader-Willi Syndrome, a rare and complex genetic birth defect that causes low muscle tone, short stature, incomplete sexual development, behavior problems, and the most bizarre characteristic of all—an uncontrollable and insatiable appetite, which causes its victims to overeat and become severely obese. People with Prader-Willi Syndrome will eat anything, including garbage. If left unsupervised, Elana would literally eat herself to death! Many people with Prader-Willi Syndrome, including Elana, are also mentally deficient.

Every time I think of abortion, I think of my precious Elana. Would it have been better if Elana had been aborted? Better for whom? In Elana's case, no one knew about her problems while she was in the womb; her condition was not diagnosed until she was three years old. But if my sister and her husband had known Elana would have all these disabilities, would they have chosen to abort her? Should they have? What is the right answer?

It would be hard to convey what this little girl has meant to our family. Her innocent and childlike ways have brought great joy to us, and she has radically changed the way we look at life and the way we live our lives. Elana's quality of life is good, too. She receives unlimited and unconditional love from all who know her and is progressing much better than many thought possible.

But some would still argue it would have been better if a child such as Elana had been aborted. Then no one would have to provide the lifetime care Elana will require, and she would not have to live her life handicapped.

Roe v. Wade

I vividly remember the now-famous 1973 *Roe v. Wade* United States Supreme Court decision that gave American women the right to choose birth or abortion for their babies. Who are we to make that decision?

In *Roe v. Wade,* the Supreme Court upheld the freedom for women to choose abortion as part of a right to privacy that is protected by the due process of the Fourteenth Amendment. Many people felt this was one of the most important pieces of legislature ever passed, and a major victory for women's rights. Its impact is still felt today, and its merits are still argued and debated. Abortion continues to be one of the most highly emotional and controversial issues in our society.

What Is Abortion?

Abortion is ending a pregnancy early before the baby is born. Sometimes a woman will abort a baby naturally (miscarry). Induced abortion, whether surgical or medicinal, is always a conscious decision—a choice—to end the life of a pre-born baby. Consequently, choosing abortion is a traumatic and agonizing decision for any woman to make. Why, then, would anyone choose to have an abortion?

Reasons for Abortion

Some women choose abortion for purely selfish reasons—a baby might interfere with her lifestyle or disrupt her career or perhaps the timing is just not right. A frightened teenage girl who may think her parents will disown her for being pregnant might think abortion is the only way out.

Many poor women say they can't afford a child. Some women become pregnant as a result of an affair, and abortion is chosen so the affair will not be exposed. Others agonize over this decision when they learn their baby may have a birth defect. Some consider abortion as an alternative if they become pregnant after having been raped.

Is abortion always wrong or are there instances when it could be justified? These are tough questions for anyone, but Christian women must get off the fence on this matter and have some convictions and principles about the emotional issue of abortion. We need to know where we stand.

How Common Is Abortion?

Recent statistics show 70 percent of women who walk into an abortion clinic say they have a church affiliation and 27 percent attend church services once a week. Even more startling is that one out of six women sitting in various church pews has experienced abortion! More than one million teenage girls in the United States—one in ten under age 20—will become pregnant this year. Forty-eight percent of them will give birth, 11 percent will miscarry, and 41 percent will decide to take the baby's life through abortion.

Since the *Roe v. Wade* decision, 26 percent of all abortions have been performed on teenagers. Something is terribly wrong when 4500 abortions are performed every day in the United States alone—1.6 million a year! Even if some try to justify abortion because of rape, incest, or to save the mother's life, those figures are astonishing and tragic!

Just a Blob of Tissue?

As uncouth and crass as the term *blob of tissue* is, these words are used by some people to describe the growing fetus. Pro-life and pro-choice advocates disagree over several aspects of abortion, but the most common argument is that a fetus is not really a human being, but just a blob of tissue.

Numerous studies refute the argument that the fetus is not a living creature. The unborn child in the womb feels pain, kicks, and takes nourishment. It has been proven that by the sixth week, the adrenal gland and the thyroid are working. By the tenth week, the fetus's appearance is so human-like that it profoundly disturbs most people to think about killing it. The child's fingerprints have formed by the twelfth week. Considering this evidence and the biblical evidence of the sacredness of life, it isn't hard to conclude that the fetus is indeed a person.

Does God Really Care?

Genesis 1:27 tells us that God is the author of life. He created us in His image and likeness; therefore human life is sacred. Who are we as human beings to decide we are smarter than God, and take it upon ourselves to terminate an inconvenient pregnancy?

But does God really consider an unborn fetus a person? The powerful verses in Psalms 139:13–16 tell us God has a special relationship with us—even before we are born! In this well-known and beautiful passage, David said:

> For You formed my inward parts; You covered me in my mother's womb. I will praise You, for I am fearfully and wonderfully made; marvelous are your works, and that my soul knows very well. My frame was not hidden from You, when I was made in secret, and skillfully wrought in the lowest parts of the earth. Your eyes saw my substance, being yet unformed. And in your book they all were written, The days fashioned for me when as yet there were none of them.

What an awesome thought! It is obvious from this scripture that God knows us before we are born. He relates to us and is personally concerned for us before birth. In Jeremiah 1:5, the Lord said, "Before I formed you in the womb, I knew you."

It is interesting, too, that biblical writers saw continuity between the prenatal and the postnatal states. To illustrate, the Hebrew word *yeled,* used of children in general, is also used of children in the womb in Exodus 21:22. The Greek word *brephos* is used in Acts 7:19 to refer to the young Hebrew children slaughtered during Pharaoh's reign and in Luke 1:41 and 44 to refer to John the Baptist while still in his mother's womb.

What Does the Bible Say about Abortion?

There is no specific command in the Bible concerning abortion, per se. However, many passages, such as the ones just mentioned, allude to the sacredness of life. Nothing could be more innocent than the blood of a developing child. We are told in Proverbs 6:16–19 that one of the seven things God hates is "hands that shed innocent blood."

In Exodus 20:13, one of the *Ten Commandments* states: "You shall not murder." This Old Testament commandment, and also commandments and examples found in the New Testament, could be clearly applied to abortion. God truly does know us before we are born, and considers us as "people."

Jesus also loved little children. Can you imagine that Christ would ever approve of aborting a child? Consider the many instances in which Jesus referred to children and showed His love, compassion, and respect for them. Listen to the words of Jesus in these well-known New Testament verses:

> Suffer little children to come unto me, and forbid them not: for of such is the kingdom of God (Luke18:16 KJV).

> Except ye be converted, and become as little children, ye shall not enter into the kingdom of heaven (Matthew 18:3 KJV).

> Whosoever therefore shall humble himself as this little child, the same is the greatest in the kingdom of heaven (Matthew 18:4 KJV).

Methods of Abortion

Although abortionists and some feminists may discount the following as merely scare tactics, let us carefully consider several methods of abortion. Regardless of whether or not our world becomes indifferent to abortion, we as Christians must never lose our conviction of what is right and wrong. We must never forget what actually occurs during an abortion.

1. *Suction Aspiration.* This is the most common abortion method and is performed during the first trimester. During this procedure, the pregnant woman's cervix is dilated and a powerful suction tube is inserted into her uterus. This suction tube rips apart the body of the developing child. The placenta, amniotic fluid, and body parts are sucked into a jar, where smaller parts of the child's body are often still recognizable.

2. *Dilation and Curettage (D&C).* During this method, the cervix is dilated and a loop-shaped knife is inserted into the uterus. The surgeon scrapes the uterus, dismembers the developing child, and then detaches the placenta from the uterine wall.

Profuse blood loss and uterine tearing are also likely to occur during this form of abortion.

3. *Prostaglandin Injections.* To induce premature labor, prostaglandin chemicals are administered to the pregnant woman orally, intravenously, or injected directly into the amniotic sac. The contractions caused by these injections are more violent than those occurring during normal delivery, so they frequently kill the baby. Some babies are even decapitated. The child is frequently born alive, although usually too small to survive.

4. *Salting (Salt Poisoning).* Although not as common today as during the '70s and '80s, salting still accounts for thousands of abortions a year. During this procedure, a long needle is inserted through the abdomen and a solution of concentrated salt is injected directly into the amniotic sac. The child breathes in the salt solution and is poisoned by it. The concentrated saline solution burns off the outer layer of the baby's skin; it often causes brain hemorrhages. It takes about an hour for the child to slowly die by this method. Approximately one day later, the woman goes into labor and delivers a dead baby.

Other Abortion Procedures

Two new controversial abortion procedures have been introduced recently. Partial-birth abortion is the most invasive and controversial of all the procedures; the other method, RU-486, is commonly referred to as the abortion pill.

- *Partial-Birth Abortion.* During this method, the abortionist uses ultrasound and forceps to pull the baby's legs into the birth canal, delivering the entire body except for the head. The abortionist then jams scissors into the back of the baby's skull and opens the scissors to enlarge the hole. A suction tube is inserted, the child's brains are vacuumed out, causing the skull to collapse. The dead baby is then removed. It's easy to understand why this is the most controversial and sickening abortion method, yet it continues to happen. It is horrifying to know that many of the fetuses are already four-and-one-half to six months old when this procedure is performed.

- *RU-486.* This newest form of abortion is hailed as a "kinder, gentler" form of abortion! Popularly known as the abortion pill, the Food and Drug Administration (FDA) approved the manufacture and use of RU-486 in the United States in October 2000. A doctor usually administers RU-486 to a woman sometimes during the first seven weeks of her pregnancy.

During this procedure, the pregnant woman is given mifepristone, a pill which causes the embryo to detach from the uterus lining. Two days later, still under the care of a doctor, the woman is given a second drug, misoprostol, which causes contractions needed to expel the embryo. Within two weeks, a third appointment with the doctor is required to confirm the abortion is complete.

It sounds nice and easy. It's private and less invasive than surgical abortion, and it's just between the patient and the doctor. No one has to know, and it's done early in the pregnancy. It's still abortion! God will know what has happened, the woman taking the abortion pills will know, and she will live forever with the knowledge that a living creature, her child, has been destroyed.

Physical Effects of Abortion

The physical dangers of abortions are often not publicized or honestly conveyed to women. Possible complications include uterine tears, cervix damage, infections, and increased risk of miscarriage in future pregnancies. Some women hemorrhage, endure severe infections, and go into shock.

National statistics on abortion show that about 10 percent of women undergoing induced abortion suffer from immediate complications. The leading causes of death from abortion during the past few years have been hemorrhage from uterine bleeding, generalized infection, and blood clots in the lungs.

Psychological Effects of Abortion

Relief is usually the only positive reaction to abortion; however, this feeling is temporary. Within eight weeks after their abortions, one survey showed that 55 percent of the women expressed guilt, 44 percent complained of nervous disorders, 36 percent experienced sleep disturbances, and 31 percent had regrets about their decision.

Another study performed by the University of Minnesota showed that five to ten years after having an abortion, 81 percent of mothers reported preoccupation and thoughts of the aborted child, 54 percent had nightmares, and an whopping 96 percent felt their abortion had taken a human life.

Research also indicates that women who have undergone post-abortion counseling report over one hundred major reactions to abortion. Among the most frequently reported are: depression, loss of self-esteem, self-destructive behavior, sleep disorders, memory loss, sexual dysfunction, chronic problems with relationships, dramatic personality change, anxiety attacks, guilt and remorse, difficulty grieving, increased tendency toward violence, chronic crying, difficulty concentrating, flashbacks, loss of interest in previously enjoyed activities and people, and difficulty in bonding with later children.

Spiritual Effects of Abortion

In addition to the devastating physical and psychological effects, many spiritual problems and issues are also brought about by abortion. Many women lose their faith in God and in others, their self-esteem is all but destroyed, and many say they hate themselves. Some end up rejecting the church, marriage, and men in general.

Special Cases?

Would abortion be an acceptable alternative when a woman has been raped or becomes pregnant through incest? Many Christians give a standard answer to the abortion issue by stating, "I think it's wrong except in cases of rape or incest, or when the mother's life is in danger." Would it be all right in those cases? Tough questions for sure! It is extremely difficult to give an unequivocal yes or no.

In his book, *Twelve Things I Want My Kids to Remember Forever,* Jerry Jenkins gives a thought-provoking and perhaps controversial reply to those questions. His opinion is that abortion would not be right under any circumstance, even for rape, incest, sexual assault, or to save the mother's life!

Although at first glance, this seems to be a harsh conclusion, the author's reasoning is that if a young woman is raped and able to conceive, she is able to have the baby. She can either have the baby and care for it or give it up through adoption to a loving family. In any case, the victim—the unborn baby—is not at fault, and the young woman would be traumatized anyway if she had an abortion. We sometimes assume, too, that rape victims who become pregnant would naturally want abortions, but in the only major study of pregnant rape victims ever done, 75 to 85 percent chose against abortion!

The writer continued his thoughts concerning abortion to save the life of the mother by making a very interesting point:

> Dr. C. Everett Koop, for years chief of staff at Philadelphia Center Children's Hospital, a renowned pediatric surgeon and eventually Surgeon General of the United States, stated that in his decades as a pediatric surgeon, he had never once seen or heard of a situation where either the mother's life or the unborn baby's life was required to be terminated to save the other. He wasn't saying it had never happened. He was saying, as probably the world's leading authority in this area, that he was unaware of it. Perhaps having to neglect the child during a trauma to attend to its mother would cost the child its life. But is there ever a reason to purposely abort that baby to save the mother? The man who should know says he's never heard of or seen it.

We may disagree with Mr. Jenkins' comments, but his words and thoughts are surely worthy of our prayerful consideration.

How Should a Christian Handle the Abortion Issue?

The easiest way to avoid having to make a decision about whether or not to have an abortion is never to get into an unwanted pregnancy. Young, unmarried Christian women must be responsible enough to set sexual limits and ground rules before starting to date. After marriage, women must continue to be responsible and spiritually mature in planning their families. Consider the following ways in which we as Christian women can address the abortion issue:

- *Oppose It.* We need to let the world know where we stand. We must know what the Bible teaches about it and not waffle or straddle the fence in our convictions about abortion.

- *Choose Life, Not Abortion.* Abortion should never be used as a birth control method! Even if an unmarried young Christian woman should find herself faced with an unwanted pregnancy, she should think long and hard before consenting to abortion.

Other options such as adoption, keeping and raising the baby, or seeking help from parents or grandparents are available.

A young lady can be forgiven for becoming pregnant even though she is not married, but young women often have a hard time ever forgiving themselves once they have an abortion. They can't go back once their baby has been aborted.

- *Be Compassionate, Not Judgmental.* Regardless of our personal opinion or convictions toward abortion, we should always exhibit a compassionate and Christ-like attitude toward those who have had an abortion.

Young woman, you must learn about abortion and the consequences of it. Abortion has been and will continue to be one of the most controversial, emotional, and explosive issues of our time. As Christian women, we would do well to remember the words of the Bible concerning the sacredness and uniqueness of life. We must continue to treat abortion as sin, hence displeasing to God. As a nation, we would do well to remember these sobering words spoken concerning America:

> America needs no words . . . to see how your decision in *Roe v. Wade* has deformed a great nation. The so-called right to abortion has pitted mothers against their children and women against men. It has portrayed the greatest of gifts—a child—as a competitor, an intrusion, and an inconvenience.

It's Your Turn!

1. When does a fetus becomes a living soul?

2. List some reasons a woman would choose to have an abortion.

3. What does the Bible say about abortion?

4. Discuss the morality of an early abortion performed to prevent the birth of a supposedly deformed child.

5. How does RU-486 terminate a pregnancy? Give a Christian's perspective on using that method.

6. Make a list of alternatives to abortion.

7. What does God expect of a woman who is pregnant because of rape?

8. What do the terms *pro-life* and *pro-choice* mean?

9. Discuss the significance of *Roe v. Wade.*

10. How would you deal with a friend who is considering abortion? How would you treat a woman who has already had an abortion?

CHAPTER FOUR

Bad Hair Days:
Liking the Way We Look

Compromising Our Individuality

Fence-Straddling Position: "Just as long as I'm beautiful—I don't need you, God!"

Bible Position: "Do not let your adornment be merely outward—arranging the hair, wearing gold, or putting on fine apparel—rather let it be the hidden person of the heart, with the incorruptible beauty of a gentle and quiet spirit, which is very precious in the sight of God" (1 Peter 3:3–4).

Scripture Search

Genesis 1:26–27, 31	Matthew 22:39
1 Samuel 16:6–7	John 3:16
Psalms 139:14	Romans 5:8
Proverbs 15:33	Romans 12:3
Proverbs 27:2	Galatians 1:15
Proverbs 31:30	1 Peter 3:3–4

Say What?

Individuality—Particular characteristics that distinguish one person from another.

Unique—One of a kind. Incomparable. Having no like or equal.

Obsession—A preoccupation with a persistent thought, action, idea, or image.

Appearance—The outward look of something or someone.

Self-confidence—Belief in ourselves to do things, to take action to change our circumstances, and to meet our goals.

Self-respect—The degree to which we think we deserve to be happy, to have rewarding relationships, and to stand up for our goals and values. Proper regard for the dignity of our own character.

Self-esteem—A favorable impression of ourselves and respect for ourselves.

Ego—Self-importance; love of self.

Comparison—Examining two or more things or people to determine similarities and differences.

Humble—Modest, courteously respectful. Not proud or arrogant. Meek and unpretentious.

As a junior in high school, Nikki was a ten. She was president of her class, active in the church youth group, an outstanding scholar athlete, and a member of the National Honor Society. Nikki never had a bad hair day—or did she?

Looking back to the summer before she began her senior year of high school, Nikki recalls: "I always felt the pressure to excel. I had to be the best at whatever I did, regardless of what it was."

Her boyfriend, Jason, star athlete with a scholarship to a prestigious university, remembers: "Nikki was so focused on doing everything right that she became obsessed with being perfect."

On a date one night, Jason casually kidded Nikki about putting on a little weight. Crushed, Nikki went on a diet with a vengeance. Then she did the unthinkable and began to gag herself after eating, thus controlling her calorie intake. Her 125-pound frame shrunk to a dangerous 98 pounds.

Her body began to sag and the glow of her once beautiful skin paled from lack of nutrition. Her weight continued to drop, yet Nikki denied there was a problem. In her attempt to be perfect and to control all aspects of her life, Nikki came dangerously close to killing herself by starving.

Months later, after intense therapy and counseling, Nikki said, "I realize my problem had a lot to do with controlling everything and my unrealistic desire to be perfect."

Nikki's weight eventually stabilized to a healthier range, but her frightening experience lowered her self-esteem and permanently damaged her body.

Growing up in a household with my two sisters and a mother who was a hairdresser, it seems as though hair has always played an important part in my life. I've worn mine shaggy, spiked, permed, short, long, flipped, curly, straight, brown, blonde, orange, and green. Some of those choices were intentional; others were definitely mistakes!

In the past, I've cried about it, I've cut it out of spite, I've thrown brushes at the mirror when it didn't look exactly right, and I've refused to go out in public because my hair did not look just the way I wanted it to look. Talk about bad hair days! As insignificant as hair seems, my sisters and I went to great lengths to get ours just right, but judging from some of our old pictures, we weren't always successful.

Regardless, the expression "bad hair day" carries with it many negative images of the ways we as women often see ourselves. Whether we're fretting over bad hair, worrying about our weight, or obsessing over our looks, it seems as though we are always searching for perfection. We struggle to keep on top of the latest fads in clothing, the best diets, and the most effective ways to exercise.

Of course, there is nothing inherently wrong with wanting to look our best and have healthy bodies, but the danger lies when we become obsessed with our physical bodies and outward appearances. This chapter deals with the ways in which women sometimes view their physical bodies. With some women, physical appearances and looks have become the top priority in their lives.

How Does God See Us?

In 1 Samuel 16:7, the biggest clue is given as to how God sees His children. When the Lord sent Samuel to the house of Jesse in Bethlehem to choose a new king of Israel, Samuel first saw Eliab, one of Jesse's handsome sons. In verses 6 and 7, we are told:

> So it was, when they came, that he [Samuel] looked at Eliab and said, "Surely the Lord's anointed is before Him." But the Lord said to Samuel, "Do not look at his appearance or at the height of his stature, because I have refused him. For the Lord does not see as man sees; for man looks at the outward appearance, but the Lord looks at the heart."

Another of Jesse's sons, the shepherd boy, David, was eventually chosen as king of Israel.

Christian women need to understand God does truly look on our hearts and spirits. He sees our inner beauty and is not so concerned with the outward appearance—whether or not we are physically beautiful. Proverbs 31:30 says that "beauty is passing, but a woman who fears the Lord shall be praised."

In the New Testament, the beautiful verses in 1 Peter 3:3–4 bring everything into proper perspective. There Peter says that braided or fancy hair, gold jewelry, or fine clothes do not make a woman beautiful; rather, our beauty comes from within. He alludes to the beauty of a "quiet and gentle spirit" which is precious in the sight of God.

How to Develop a Spirit that God Loves

How can we in the twenty-first century develop this quiet and gentle spirit so loved by God? How do we stop being appearance obsessed? Here are five practical suggestions that will help each of us develop a healthy self-image.

1. *Stop Comparing Yourself with Others.* How much time do you waste obsessing over things about which you can do nothing—big hips, skinny legs, small eyes? The more you compare your looks to others, the more dissatisfied you become with your own appearance, and the more dissatisfied you are with your appearance, the more likely you are to seek confirmation from others that you look okay.

   All of us are inclined to compare ourselves either "upwardly" or "downwardly." If we compare ourselves to someone who is not as good as we think we are, it will be easy for us to develop a haughty and arrogant attitude. On the other hand, if we constantly compare ourselves to those who we think are better than ourselves or prettier than we are, we may begin to feel sorry for ourselves and suffer low self-esteem. Either way we lose. The comparison game is always a no-win situation.

2. *Start Feeling Good about Yourself from the Inside Out.* Instead of eating compulsively, dieting, and exercising excessively, ponder the words of David in Psalms 139:14, when he said we are "fearfully and wonderfully made." We can better understand this expression by discovering how our bodies work—what makes us tick. By eating sensibly, exercising reasonably, and enjoying pure physical activity, we can appreciate the marvelous and wonderful ways our bodies work, not just how they look.

3. *Stop Obsessing over Weight.* In her book, *Appearance Obsession, Learning to Love the Way You Look,* Dr. Joni Johnson states that "fatism," discrimination based on body size, often begins early. She states:

   > Children develop an active dislike of obesity by age six, and by age seven have acquired ideal perceptions of attractiveness. By age ten, their prejudice against obesity is firmly in place.

   As adults, one of the hardest things to unlearn in our culture is our prejudice against people who are overweight. Fatism thrives in today's society, but we need to adjust our attitudes toward weight and make peace with our bodies. This is not to say that we should "let ourselves go," but too often we are obsessed with the impossible task of obtaining the perfect weight.

4. *Develop a Healthy Love of Self.* God expects you to love your-self. In Matthew 22:37–38 Jesus said the first and greatest commandment is to love the Lord God with all our heart, soul, and mind. Verse 39 says, "The second is like it: You shall love your neighbor as yourself." It's clear we must first love our-selves before we can love others! Jane McWhorter makes an excellent point concerning loving ourselves:

> Self love is not conceit or arrogance. It is the acceptance of yourself with the same love and tolerance of your shortcomings that you desire God and others to exhibit toward you!

Healthy self-love is scriptural, and there is nothing wrong with loving ourselves. After learning to love ourselves, then we can genuinely know how to love others.

5. *Strive for Humility.* You should indeed love yourself as Christ commanded, but also remember that nothing is more unattractive and unlike Christ than being conceited, vain, self-centered, and appearance obsessed. We don't talk much about modesty and humility today, but maybe we should, since they are qualities most characteristic of Christ Himself.

While we are expected to love ourselves, we should never think we are better than we are. In Romans 12:3, Paul admon-ished us not to think more highly of ourselves than we ought to think, "but to think soberly, as God has dealt to each one a measure of faith." In verse 10, he continues, "Be kindly affec-tionate to one another with brotherly love, in honor giving preference to one another." Philippians 2:3–5 says our atti-tude should be the same as exhibited by Jesus Christ—that of humility. Verses 3 and 4 say:

> Let nothing be done through selfish ambition or conceit, but in lowli-ness of mind let each esteem others better than himself. Let each of you look out not only for his own interests, but also for the interest of others.

How can we do that? One good way is to associate with those we might not initially consider to be worthy of our friendship. In other words, make friends with those who seem unimportant. Also, always strive to be humble and never think of yourself as smarter or better than you actually are. Romans 12:16 says, "Be of the same mind toward one another. Do not set your mind on high things, but associate with the humble. Do not be wise in your own opinion."

The book of Proverbs is filled with references to living modestly and humbly. Proverbs 6:17 tells us that one of the things the Lord hates is a proud or haughty look. Christians should be humble people. Proverbs 27:2 says: "Let another man praise you, and not your own mouth; a stranger, and not your own lips." In Proverbs 15:33, we are told that "the fear of the Lord is the instruction of wisdom. And before honor is humility." Genuine modesty and humility are the building blocks for developing a quiet and gentle spirit that is so loved by God.

Self-Esteem

The root problem of appearance obsession, like many other maladies we bring upon ourselves, is a poor self-image, resulting in low self-esteem. Judging from the number of books in our libraries and on the bookshelves, self-esteem appears to be the most popular subject of our day. Book after book attempts to explain what it is, how to get it, how to keep it—and the list goes on and on. Low self-esteem has been blamed for nearly every problem imaginable in today's society.

If we could just see, though, low self-esteem doesn't make us appealing to others at all, and it can become the height of self-occupation and self-importance, which the Bible speaks out against! People who dislike themselves are not really humble at all, since they continually concentrate on themselves and their supposed lack of worth. In contrast, people who like themselves aren't always dwelling on themselves, but thinking of others.

Often when we suffer from low self-esteem, we spend all our time thinking others are being critical of us or that every slight remark is directed specifically to us. We can become so absorbed and occupied with ourselves that all we can think about is ourselves! The Bible is clear, though, that we are to think of others. In Matthew 16:24, Jesus said we must deny ourselves if we are to be His true followers.

Going to the Extreme

In attempts to make our physical bodies attractive, we do some-times go the extreme. Notice some of the ways we tend to go over-board.

- *Dieting*—Recent surveys indicate that up to 25 percent of seven-year-old girls have attempted to lose weight. These little girls are only imitating what they see in adult women. Doc-tors tell us that most eating disorders begin between the ages of nine and eleven.

  Our society has become prejudiced against people who are overweight—and the younger ones see that. As it did with Nikki, dieting may lead girls and young women to the painful and deadly practices of anorexia (self-starvation) and bulimia (purging oneself with laxatives and vomiting after eating large quantities of food).

  According to the National Association of Anorexia Nervosa and Associated Eating Disorders, roughly seven million Ameri-can girls and women (and one million boys and men) struggle with eating disorders. The mortality rate from anorexia is estimated between 10 and 20 percent and is the highest of any mental disorder.

- *Excessive Exercising*—Throughout my life I have attempted to stay fit by regularly exercising in some way, but I've often wondered if I've done more damage than good when I con-sider the pulled muscles, torn ligaments, aching joints, and broken bones I've experienced from excessive exercising over the years. Of course, there are many good reasons to exercise regularly, and the benefits of moderate exercise are well docu-mented.

  Exercise can help reduce the risks of stroke, heart disease, osteoporosis, diabetes, and other diseases. It has been proved to have many emotional benefits, such as helping to alleviate depression and anxiety. However, too much of a good thing can hurt both our bodies and our relationships, if we use excessive or extreme forms of exercising as a way of escaping bad relationships or to shape our bodies into something they weren't meant to be.

- *Youth Worship*—American culture emphasizes youth and beauty. As women, we suffer from an unrealistic expectation that we should look like movie stars or athletes, but we may be disappointed as the years roll by and our youth and beauty fades. It's sad, but true, that women in our society are often viewed less attractive as they age. But older women can be beautiful! The beauty of a quiet and gentle spirit and the contentment, wisdom, and peacefulness many older women exhibit are worthy goals for all young Christian women. Proverbs 15:30 teaches that our beauty and happiness will show in our eyes.

Variety—The Spice of Life

In Genesis 1:26–27, we are told that God created both male and female in His image and likeness. Verse 31 tells us God looked on everything He had made and saw that it was very good. God didn't make any junk—we are all unique and special individuals, beautiful in God's sight!

Variation is a great gift from God, and what a boring world it would be if everyone acted the same and looked the same. Once we learn to accept what we can't change and make peace with our looks, we will be on our way to a more peaceful and happy existence.

When we remember God loved us so much that He gave His Son to die for us, it will be difficult to ever feel insignificant. What an awesome gift! Ruth Senter said,

> I wonder how our lives might look if we were as content with ourselves as God is with us. I wonder how different things might be if we relearned what contentment is all about. If we refused to believe we have to be something bigger, brighter, bolder than we are. If we took the pressure off ourselves by no longer having to prove ourselves significant. If we simply believed that we *are* significant.

Lessons Learned from "Bad Hair"

Hopefully, we can all learn something from our bad hair days. When bad hair days appear from nowhere, keep these thoughts and analogies about hair in mind and resolve to do the best you can in your particular situation, whatever that may be.

- *People Don't Notice It As Much As You Do.* We would be surprised to learn that no one pays as much attention to our hair—

or to ourselves in general—as we ourselves do or as much as we think others do. We're often impressed by our own importance. Remember this one to avoid pride and in promoting our own self-importance. It will keep our egos from swelling.

- *Someone Else's Hair Will Always Look Better Than Yours.* Playing the comparison game is a sure way to damage our egos and deflate our self-images. The comparison game is a no-win situation. This thought will keep us humble.

- *You Might Not Be Able to Change It Instantly.* Have you ever had a hairstyle that ended up a little too short, a little too curly, or the wrong color? Then you can identify with this one! We may not be able to change our hair or our circumstances overnight, but we can accept our situation for the time being and do the best we can with it. This thought will teach us patience.

- *It'll Grow Back.* It's not the end of the world, and things are not as bad as they seem, even with a haircut that got a little out of hand! The hair will grow back, regardless of what we may think when we first look in the mirror and gasp. And life goes on, regardless of what we think about a lot of our circumstances. This analogy will teach us to have a sense of humor.

- *It's Gonna Go Out of Style.* So why not try new things? Remember this one in learning to reach out and try something new. Change is good, even though it may not always be easy.

- *It Always Looks Best the Day Before You Get It Cut.* Most women know our hair always looks its best, and we get the most compliments about it the day before our haircut is scheduled. Canceling the appointment is a sure mistake. Get it cut anyway! This thought will teach us to go with our instinct and have a little confidence in our own opinion.

- *It'll Never Be Perfect.* There are no perfect hair days in life just as there are no perfect days in general, so the sooner we learn this, the happier we'll be!

Beauty Tips for a Young Christian Woman

Regardless of the pressure to conform to a certain standard in today's society as far as fashion, weight, or looks go, we as Christian women can stand out from the world by looking to the Bible as our guide in setting the proper standards for our own style and inner beauty. Romans 12:2 is a well-known verse that tells Christians not to be conformed or molded to this world, but to be changed from within by a new way of thinking. This beauty of a quiet and gentle spirit will stand the test of time and will show in the way we carry ourselves, in our smiles and eyes, and in our daily walks of life.

As a teenager, the famous actress Audrey Hepburn was a courier for the *Belgian Underground Anti-Nazi Movement* during World War II. She offered these excellent beauty tips:

- For attractive lips: Speak words of kindness.
- For lovely eyes: Seek out the good in people.
- For a slim figure: Share your food with the hungry.
- For beautiful hair: Let a child run his or her fingers through it once a day.
- For poise: Walk with the knowledge you'll never walk alone.

The beauty of a woman is not in the clothes she wears, the figure she maintains, or in the way she combs her hair. The beauty of a woman is seen in her eyes, because that is the doorway to her heart, the place where love resides. True beauty in a woman is reflected in her soul. It is the care that she lovingly gives, the passion that she shows. And the beauty of a woman only grows with passing years.

It's Your Turn!

1. What does the expression "bad hair day" mean to you personally?

2. Why do young people, especially girls, have a problem with anorexia and bulimia?

3. What does the Bible say about outward appearances versus inward appearances?

4. How can a person be attractive without being appearance obsessed?

5. What are some ways you can develop a healthy attitude toward your body?

6. Why is the comparison game so easy when it comes to our looks?

7. How does society judge the appearance of older women?

8. List some ways you can love others as you love yourself.

9. What does it mean to be humble?

10. What are some ways we can "esteem others better" than ourselves? (Philippians 2:3.)

CHAPTER FIVE

I Never Meant to Hurt Anyone!

Compromising Our Character

Fence-Straddling Position: "So I've got a little temper problem—so what? It's really no big deal."

Bible Position: "So then, my beloved brethren, let every man be swift to hear, slow to speak, slow to wrath; for the wrath of man does not produce the righteousness of God" (James 1:19–20).

Scripture Search

Proverbs 6:16–19	Matthew 12:36–37
Proverbs 15:1–2	Colossians 3:8
Proverbs 25:11	1 Timothy 4:11–12
Proverbs 26:20	1 Timothy 5:13
Proverbs 27:2	James 1:19–20
Ecclesiastes 5:1–7	James 1:26
Isaiah 53:7	James 3:5–10

Say What?

Character—Who we are on the inside—who we are when no one is looking.

Reputation—What others think of us.

Disposition—Temperament. Mental outlook or mood.

Profanity—Language characterized by irreverence for God or sacred things.

Gossip—Idle talk or rumor, especially about the personal or private affairs of others.

Blasphemy—Profanity, cursing, or speaking irreverently of God and spiritual things. Assuming to oneself the rights or qualities of God.

Slander—A malicious and false statement about someone.

Slang—Very informal speech and writing characterized by the use of vulgar and socially taboo language.

Bridle—To bring under control or restraint.

Encourage—To inspire with spirit and confidence. To uplift by approval and reassurance.

"Whitney, how about a quick nine holes of golf tomorrow?" It was Catherine, Whitney's co-worker.

"Sounds good to me! My new clubs need a good workout."

"Great, I'll meet you at the municipal course in the morning around nine o'clock. I'm looking forward to it."

Saturday morning dawned bright and cool with blue skies and a light wind—perfect golf weather.

"Catherine, check out my new driver—it's a beauty, don't you think?" said Whitney.

"Yeah, it looks great. You should be able to hit that little white ball a mile with that!" laughed Catherine.

"Okay, here goes, then!" Whitney said as she lined up for her first shot.

"Crack!" *the driver smacked the ball. Catherine remained quiet as Whitney's first ball flew deep into the woods.*

Whitney struck the ground with her new driver. "Well, that was lousy! I'm going to hit a mulligan, if you don't mind," *she said.*

"Sure, go ahead," *agreed Catherine.*

"Smack!" *Whitney's ball sliced into a small pond.*

Whitney slammed her club onto the ground. "Well, looks like it's going to be one of those days," *she muttered under her breath.*

Things quickly went from bad to worse. As they approached the third hole, Whitney had already lost six balls. She lined up to hit her seventh ball; another golf ball sailed into a thick grove of trees.

"I've had it! This stupid club! I can't do anything right! I hate this stupid game!" *Whitney screamed. She suddenly grabbed the driver, gave it a good baseball swing, and turned it loose.*

"Whup, whup, whup!" *screeched the airborne club.*

Catherine ducked. The club barely missed her head as it flew off onto the fairway.

"Whoa!" *Catherine called as Whitney ran after her club.* "I thought this was just a friendly little match between us. I didn't know you would take it so seriously!"

"Well, you thought wrong," *Whitney called over her shoulder. She retrieved the driver and in one motion, broke it over her knee.* "If I can't do any better than this, I'm just gonna quit."

"Well, that's fine with me, too," *Catherine said.* "Go ahead and quit. I'm outta here."

Catherine quickly gathered up her clubs and abruptly started for her car.

"I'm sorry . . . I didn't mean it!" *Whitney began to apologize, as she ran after her friend.* "Wait! Stop! Please!" *But she was too late. Catherine got into her car and drove away.*

Well, I've done it again, I've hurt another friend. I'm supposed to be the Christian here, and look what I've done. What am I going to do with this temper? . . . I've done it again, I've done it again . . . *her mind repeated as she walked, head down, to the car.*

My favorite verse in the New Testament is James 1:19. I've read it hundreds of times—mainly because I need to reinforce it in my life, and I need to practice it. We all do. Condensed, it simply says, "This you know, my beloved brethren. But let everyone be quick to hear, slow to speak and slow to anger." Three separate statements, yet all so tied together in three great lessons.

Can you relate to Whitney's temper problem? Looking back on my own life, I remember times I've destroyed things in fits of anger, too, just because they didn't work right. I'm not proud of these things, just painfully aware of a temper with a short fuse. Thankfully, my anger is nearly always directed toward some inanimate object such as weed eaters and lawn mowers, and not at other people!

Regardless, these little displays of temper are not pretty for anyone, and they don't help a thing either. Solomon addressed the temper problem in Proverbs 14:29 when he said: "He who is slow to anger has great understanding, but he who is quick-tempered exalts folly" (NASB). It's as true today as it was in Solomon's day.

Anger itself is not necessarily bad. Anger is just an emotion like joy or sadness, but how we react to it is so important. Looking at examples from the Bible, we see that Jesus and God both displayed anger at times. Remember the story in Matthew 21:12–13 where Jesus' anger caused Him to drive out the moneychangers from the temple? His anger moved Him to take action. Anger that is handled correctly will cause us to also take action in a loving way, not in a spiteful and hateful manner.

Lashing out in anger toward other people often leads to revenge and damages strong friendships. Once damaged, these relationships are extremely hard to mend. As Christian women we must always be aware of things (or people) that trigger our anger and learn to handle the situation in a Christ-like manner.

Hiding anger or trying to ignore it is not healthy. Suppressed anger can lead to resentment and revenge, and it also can affect our health. The Bible, however, does indicate that Christians can be angry sometimes. Ephesians 4:26 says, "Be angry, and do not sin." The same verse also admonishes Christians to get over it quickly and not to be angry too long: "Do not let the sun go down on your wrath."

Admitting anger and working out a personal method to resolve that anger are positive steps in handling trying situations. Praying to God about it keeps the anger from festering and turning into an ugly trait. The most effective way in dealing with angry words spoken directly toward us is taught in Proverbs 15:1. There Solomon simply says: "A soft answer turns away wrath, but a harsh word stirs up anger." Think about it.

Profanity

Besides temper problems, crude and hurtful language has also become a problem with many people, including Christians. When did vulgar language and cursing become so popular? It seems to be everywhere today—at the ballpark, at school, and in our neighborhoods.

How things have changed since the days of Rhett and Scarlett! Back in 1939, the movie *Gone with the Wind* was released with five bad words, including the infamous line, "Frankly, my dear. I don't—." In 1987, Mel Gibson's movie, *Lethal Weapon,* had 149 bad words. In 1999, the cartoon movie *Southpark: Bigger, Longer and Uncut*, was released with such foul language that it earned an NC-17 rating, later reduced to R after reluctant cuts by the producers.

A 1999 study by the Center for Media and Public Affairs showed that profanity is used every three minutes in major motion pictures, every two minutes on cable TV, and once every six minutes on prime-time TV shows. No wonder we no longer flinch when hearing profanity.

Today's music also pushes the limits of what constitutes acceptable language. Some of the music contains language that not only promotes violence, but also contains words of sexual explicitness and things that 20 or 30 years ago would never have been spoken about, but are solidly mainstream today.

Rap singer Eminem raps about his idea of a good time—raping his mother and abusing his wife! In his so-called music, he has also consistently made derogatory and demeaning comments about blacks, homosexuals, and women. As shocking as this is, Eminem is not shunned by many of the world or made to feel ashamed about his language or message in any way. In fact, he was rewarded for his accomplishments in 2001 with four Grammy nominations, winning one for Best Rap Album.

What about Christians? Is our language any better? How is it that Christians, especially young people, have come to use profanity and blasphemy? As wrong as it is, it appears this problem has been around forever. The third commandment of the *Ten Commandments* forbade taking God's name in vain, but there's no indication the Israelites ever stopped.

Evidently, it was common during the early days of Christianity, too. In James 3:10, James said to the Christians scattered throughout the world: "Out of the same mouth proceed blessing and cursing. My brethren, these things ought not to be so." It happened then, and it continues to happen today. The respect and reverence that should be shown toward God has been lost.

Some argue that slang and profanity spoken by young people is just that—slang, not to be taken so literally. What difference does it make? It seems to be more socially acceptable to use profanity today than it used to be, but cursing is similar to other sins that start innocently enough and with time becomes progressive. The slang soon takes on a life or tongue of its own, and before long, profanity will flow from our tongues just as easily as any other words.

Years ago, cursing was seen as a way of "being one of the boys" with men; it wasn't quite as acceptable for women. There was a time when a man would politely refrain from certain language because a woman was in his presence. How old-fashioned that seems, since the language that flows from the lips of many women today could truly make a sailor blush!

Surely a person must have a limited vocabulary if he always resorts to cursing and profanity to express his views. Some psychologists say cursing and obscene language reflects personal insecurity, and sometimes it is used merely to get attention. At other times, such language is used as an effort to be accepted or to just fit in.

Whatever the reason for using it, profanity is a sure way to damage our reputations and lose our effectiveness as Christians. We must decide to take a stand against it by using words of intelligence and gentleness, not those of cursing, profanity, and anger. It can make a huge difference in the influence we all have for Jesus Christ.

Gossip—A Woman Thing?

For some reason, women have long been perceived as more likely to gossip than men. Whether or not this is true is debatable, but evidently this thinking goes back to the early days of Christianity. Nancy Eichman in her book, *Seasoning Your Words,* offers these interesting observations concerning women and gossiping:

> Although some people may class it as relatively harmless, gossip is placed beside murder, sexual impurity, and God hating in Romans 1:29–32. A man can be disqualified from serving as a deacon if his wife is a gossip (1 Timothy 3:11). Younger widows were advised to remarry so they would not go from house to house and become gossips and busybodies (1 Timothy 5:13).

Gossiping is serious business. Idle and careless words may injure feelings, damage reputations, and destroy spirits forever. How does it feel to be the target of gossip? Women must be extra careful not to be perceived as gossips and that our words do not reflect a negative image of Christ and His followers.

Lying

Lying is mentioned in Proverbs 6:16–19 as one of seven things the Lord hates. Revelation 21:8 warns that "all liars shall have their part in the lake which burns with fire and brimstone." In spite of these strong warnings, the practice of lying has become epidemic. Some surveys indicate as many as 90 percent of Americans are not truthful under certain circumstances.

Christians are not immune either. Although we may seldom tell big lies, we often embellish our stories to make ourselves look better. We may also twist our words so they will sound less offensive and incriminating, but in doing so we may not project their true meaning. Is homosexuality really just an alternative lifestyle and is abortion merely a terminated pregnancy? Remember, the devil is behind all lying, and Jesus says in John 8:44 that Satan is the father of all lies.

Paul said in Colossians 3:9–10: "Do not lie to one another, since you have put off the old man with his deeds and have put on the new man who is renewed in knowledge according to the image of Him who create him." Ephesians 4:25 urges us to be truthful: "Therefore, putting away lying, 'let each one of you speak truth with his neighbor,' for we are members of one another."

Cheating

Is cheating a big deal? Apparently, many young people don't think so. Eighty percent of students who rank among the top of their class have cheated, and half of them agree that it's no big deal. Cheating is just a form of lying, and notice how seriously God considers lying. We just read in Revelation 21:8 that "all liars shall have their part in the lake which burns with fire and brimstone, which is the second death."

Seven in ten students surveyed admitted to cheating on a test at least once in the past year, and nearly half said they had done so more than once. Ninety-two percent of 8600 students surveyed lied to their parents in the past year. Seventy-eight percent said they had lied to a teacher, and more than one in four said they would lie to get a job.

Some students are emailing test questions and papers to each other, downloading research papers from websites, or exchanging them through news groups. Some use Palm Pilots to beam answers to each other in the classroom.

The major factor in the rise in cheating appears to be the competition for grades and the best schools following high school graduation. The mentality of "I have to have the best grades, regardless of what I'm learning" needs to be addressed by every young person; young Christian women should make the decision early to avoid the easy way out—the road of cheating.

Turn It Around!

After seeing all the negative ways in which we can express anger and hurt others with our tongues, let's look at the positive side of using our words. What a joy it is when our temper is under control and our words are used to encourage, uplift, and express love and appreciation to others! Quite simply, our words are very powerful. Proverbs 18:21 says, "Death and life are in the power of the tongue." As Christian young women, our words and kind attitudes can be used as tremendous examples of Christ and as a source of love to others.

Words of Encouragement and Praise

It has been said that a person's own name is the sweetest sound that person can hear. Everyone loves to be acknowledged and praised for a job well done or for doing her best at some particular activity. Speaking uplifting words and writing a thoughtful note are excellent ways to show love and to encourage others. I have been amazed by the kind words spoken to me by those to whom I have sent cards of encouragement. It may not seem to be a big deal, but people often cherish those cards and letters of encouragement for years.

Even though email and quick phone calls provide means by which we can thank others for their kindness or tell them we are thinking of them, it seems nothing takes the place of a good, old-fashioned handwritten note of thanks or encouragement or a simple pat on the back. Those are things almost anyone can do.

It is so important, too, for every group to have an encourager. Throughout the book of Acts, we continue to read about a man who was called a great encourager. In Acts 4:36; 9:27; 11:24; and 15:35–41, we learn that the man Joseph was such an effective encourager that he earned the nickname of Barnabas, which means "son of encouragement."

Barnabas' actions and words were crucial during the days of the early church. Imagine how the local Christians must have felt when they heard that Paul was arriving in Jerusalem. They must have been very reluctant to welcome the infamous persecutor. Yet Barnabas was willing to risk his reputation and his life to stand up for Paul and to convince the new Christians that Paul was a changed man and a believer in Christ. We can only wonder what would have happened to Paul without the encouragement Barnabas must have given to him.

Often there is a tendency to criticize rather than encourage. Our influence and our effectiveness on others concerning our belief in Jesus is greatly enhanced by being encouragers. In Acts 11:24, it is said of Barnabas: "He was a good man, full of the Holy Spirit and of faith. And a great many people were added to the Lord." Who knows the influence for good we can have on others just by encouraging them?

Don't Give Up!

Once a group of frogs was traveling through the woods, when two of them fell into a deep pit. All the other frogs gathered around the pit, and when they saw how deep it was, they shouted to the unfortunate frogs that they would never get out. The two frogs ignored the comments and tried to jump out of the pit anyway.

The other frogs kept yelling and making a great commotion, telling them to stop, that they were as good as dead. Finally, one of the frogs took heed to what the other frogs were saying and simply gave up. He lay down and died.

The other frog continued to jump as hard as he could. Once again, the crowd of frogs made a great commotion and continued to yell at him to stop the pain and suffering and just die. He jumped even harder and finally made it out of the pit.

When he got out, the other frogs tried to ask him, "Why did you continue jumping? Didn't you hear us?" The frog stared at them and tried to understand their frantic motions. He finally explained to them that he was deaf. He thought they had been cheering him on and encouraging him the entire time.

That story teaches us two lessons. Number one, there is power of life and death in the tongue. An encouraging word to someone who is down can lift them up and help them make it through the day. And, number two, a destructive word to someone who is down can be what it takes to kill him. It's a special individual who will take the time to encourage another.

Encouragement can change lives for the better, and lack of encouragement can cause frustration and feelings of inadequacy and worthlessness. Celeste Holm summed it up nicely with this thought: "We live by encouragement and die without it—slowly, sadly, and angrily."

Kind and Caring Words

Paul wrote in Ephesians 4:32: "And be kind to one another, tenderhearted, forgiving one another, just as God in Christ forgave you." Speaking hateful, rude, and sarcastic words to our loved ones and friends always cuts deeply, and the tone of our voices sometimes means more than the actual words themselves. Verse after verse in the Bible warns of the dangers of misusing our tongues and the beauty of using our words to uplift others and to praise God.

Proverbs 15:26 teaches us that the Lord hates evil thoughts, but is pleased with kind words. The apostle Paul expressed this eloquently in Colossians 4:6: "Let your speech always be with grace, seasoned with salt, that you may know how you ought to answer each one." We can be pleasing to God and kind to others by choosing our words carefully.

Listening and Laughter

Our ability to refrain from talking is also important in connecting with others. Listening has become a lost art, but it can be of great significance in relating to those who may be in need. Most people find it easier to talk and offer advice to others than to sit with them and just listen. Yet listening to another is one of the most effective ways of empathizing with them.

Numerous studies have shown laughter has great psychological and physical benefits. It can also lift our spirits and the spirits of those around us. Proverbs 17:22 says a cheerful heart is like good medicine. Humor can have a down side, though, if we laugh at others or make fun of them, instead of laughing with them. We need to guard against sarcastic comments that may send the wrong message to others.

Christ's Supreme Example

Even though Jesus showed anger in dealing with shameful and insulting conduct exhibited toward His Father, His behavior also showed us how we should handle our own anger, disappointments, and frustrations. Christ was criticized and rejected by men. Surely He was oppressed and disappointed by much He saw while on the earth, but the attitude He showed before His death gives all of us an example to follow in conducting ourselves in a Christlike manner today.

Isaiah prophesied of Christ in Isaiah 53:7:

> He was oppressed and He was afflicted, yet He opened not His mouth; He was led as a lamb to the slaughter, and as a sheep before its shearers is silent, so He opened not His mouth.

What humility and what a supreme example for us even today.

It's Your Turn!

1. Why do people curse?

2. Why is using slang a dangerous practice?

3. What are some healthy ways to handle anger?

4. Why is it so important that church leaders have wives who are not busybodies and who do not gossip?

5. Discuss the statement: "The two main reasons we lie are usually rooted in either fear or pride."

6. Why does society view women as gossips more so than men?

7. What does it mean to bridle your tongue? (James 3:2.)

8. What are some positive ways to use our tongues?

9. Why is it easier to talk than listen?

10. How did Jesus handle criticism and rejection?

CHAPTER SIX

Homosexuality: Anything But Gay
Compromising Our Tolerance for Sin

Fence-Straddling Position: "Gay people aren't hurting any-one—they're just living an alternate lifesyle."

Bible Position: "Do you not know that the unrighteous will not inherit the kingdom of God? Do not be deceived. Neither fornicators, nor idolaters, nor adulterers, nor homosexuals, nor sodomites, nor thieves, nor covetous, nor drunkards, nor revilers, nor extortioners will inherit the kingdom of God" (1 Corinthians 6:9–10).

Scripture Search

Genesis 19:1-6   Romans 1:24-32
Leviticus 18:22   1 Corinthians 6:9-11
Leviticus 20:13   Galatians 5:19-21
1 Timothy 1:9-10

Say What?

Tolerance—Sympathy toward beliefs or practices differing from one's own beliefs.

Homosexuality—Sexual behavior directed toward a person of one's own sex.

Sodomy—Unnatural sexual relations, especially anal intercourse.

Gay—Slang term for homosexuality.

Straight—Heterosexual.

Lesbian—Female homosexual.

Butch, Dyke—Slang term for the partner in a lesbian relationship who assumes the dominant role, usually the more masculine role.

Femme—Slang term for the partner in a lesbian relationship who assumes the more passive role. Opposite of butch.

Fag, Fairy, Queen—Derogatory terms for male homosexuals.

Queer—Slang, usually derogatory, for homosexual.

Homophobic—Being unreasonably afraid of homosexuals.

Celibate—Abstaining from sexual relations.

Monogamous—Having only one sexual partner.

Closet—Figurative description of a place where homosexuals hide their sexuality from the public.

Coming Out—Revealing one's homosexuality to the public. Living a homosexual lifestyle out in the open—coming out of the closet.

It was Sunday evening after worship and 17-year-old Nicole grabbed Sara's hand and pulled her into a classroom.

"Sara—do you have minute?" Anxiety trembled in her voice and pulled creases across her face.

Sara was somewhat puzzled, but she motioned for Nicole to sit down. "What's on your mind, Nicole?"

"Uh, well..." stammered Nicole. "I know we talked about this in the class you taught, and you're not going to believe it if I tell you."

"Try me," said Sara, her curiosity brimming.

"I—I—er—uh . . . I think I'm gay!" Nicole blurted it out, her eyes cast downward. "I'm afraid you're going to be upset with me, but I can't help it. I've got to be true to my feelings."

"What makes you think you're gay? And when did this happen?"

"Well," Nicole paused a moment. "I don't know when it happened. I don't know how to explain it. I just seem to feel closer to girls than I do to boys. They're so much easier to talk to, and I really don't understand those guys anyway."

"Nicole, if that's all you're going on, join the club," Sara replied reassuringly. "I don't understand guys either—but I'm not gay! Surely, there's more to it than that."

Nicole fidgeted with her necklace and then took the plunge: "Yeah, Sara, there's a lot more to it than that. I have a girlfriend and I'm in love. I think a lot of you, and I just wanted someone's approval, someone to say it's okay, and I wanted to hear that from you—but looks like I'm not gonna get it! I can tell by the look on your face you don't approve. I really don't understand what's so wrong with loving another person! Who cares if it's another girl? I'm not hurting anyone!"

Nicole began to cry; then she spoke defiantly: "What's so wrong with it? I know a little about the Bible, too, you know. Jesus never even mentioned homosexuality! How can this be wrong?"

"Just take it easy, Nicole." Sara said evenly. "Let's talk some more . . ."

Homosexuality is alive and well today wherever we may live. According to the U.S. Census figures released in August 2000, gay men and women live in 99.3 percent of all American counties and 600,000 gay and lesbian "families" currently reside in the United States. Homosexuals are in our workplaces, in our schools, within our families, and in the church. We are only fooling our-selves if we think otherwise.

While there is certainly no reason for Christians to fear, ridi-cule, or hate homosexuals, we must be aware of a great danger that lies within our society today in our increasing tolerance of homosexuality. Many homosexual relationships, especially lesbian, appear normal on the surface, so it can be easy to blend in with the world and forget that these alternative lifestyles, as popu-larly called, are actually displeasing to God and condemned by the Bible. As Christians, our love for all people, including those practicing homosexuality, should motivate us to talk with them honestly about the condition of their souls and the sinfulness of their relationships. If we don't go to them, who will?

What Is Homosexuality?

Quite simply, homosexuality is the practice of men having sexual relations with men and women having sexual relations with women. Homosexual behavior has been around for centu-ries. The most commonly referenced Bible story concerning homo-sexuality is that of Sodom and Gomorrah (Genesis 19:5–6). God destroyed those cities, in part, because of their sinful homosexual activity.

Sometimes young women worry they may be homosexual because they have a close girlfriend. Friendship should not be confused with homosexuality! The Bible tells of one of the stron-gest and most intense friendships ever between two men—David and Jonathan. In 2 Samuel 1:26, David says, "I am distressed for you, my brother Jonathan; you have been very pleasant to me; your love to me was wonderful, surpassing the love of women."

Were David and Jonathan homosexual? No! Homosexual acts were absolutely forbidden in Israel. Leviticus 18:22 and 20:13 call homosexuality abominable and detestable, even to the point of issuing a death decree on those who practiced it. David was sim-ply emphasizing the deep brotherhood and faithful friendship he had with Jonathan. There is nothing wrong with having a close, best friend of the same sex.

Why Study Homosexuality?

Christians today need to be aware of a very powerful, highly organized gay rights movement underway in our society. This political movement has the potential to change current laws and influence our attitudes toward homosexuality. In early 2000, Vermont became the first state to recognize gay unions by passing a law granting those in homosexual marriages many of the same privileges as those in heterosexual ones.

Gay activists try to paint a picture of stability in homosexual relationships quite similar to that of heterosexual marriages. Almost any honest homosexual will admit—and statistics back it up—that few gay relationships are monogamous, and most homosexuals do not remain faithful to one partner, or even several, in their lifetime.

Even if one were to argue that heterosexual marriages are also marked by adultery and divorce, homosexual relationships—in most cases—are fleeting and unstable. Promiscuity abounds in the homosexual world, even though some will argue it is no more so than in the straight world. Although HIV, AIDS, and other sexually transmitted diseases are not strictly homosexual diseases, they occur much more frequently among homosexuals than among heterosexuals.

It's no wonder, considering these astounding statistics concerning homosexual practices presented by Thomas E. Schmidt in his book *Straight and Narrow: Candor and Compassion in the Homosexual Debate:*

> Seventy-four percent of male homosexuals reported having more than 100 partners in their lifetime; 41 percent reported having more than 500 partners; and 28 percent reported having more than 1000 partners! To contrast, only two percent of lesbians reported having more than 100 partners, but 60 percent did report having at least 10 lifetime partners.

Christian women need to be aware of the growing homosexual rights movement and get off the fence in our attitudes and tolerance of this so-called gay lifestyle. If not, the day will come quickly when same-sex unions are accepted by society the same as traditional heterosexual marriages and are no longer considered rare, but commonplace.

How Common Is Homosexuality?

For years, there has been a pat answer that 10 percent of the world's population is homosexual. This figure was derived from an incorrect interpretation of statistics presented in the 1948 Kinsey Sex Report. Careful examination of the entire report shows more accurately that only four percent of the male participants and two percent of the female considered themselves homosexual over the course of a lifetime. Somehow, the 10 percent figure that Kinsey reported—among prison inmates—took on a life of its own over the years and made the assumed practice of homosexuality appear much more normal than it actually is.

Using the 2000 U.S. census of approximately 280 million people, and the 10 percent figure, we could assume there are 28 million homosexuals in the United States; using the 4 percent figure, that number drops to slightly more than 11 million. While still a significant number, there is quite a difference in 28 million and 11 million. The number of admitted homosexuals is indeed growing as their lifestyle becomes more accepted and tolerated, but the practice is still less prevalent than the gay activists would have us believe.

Why Is Homosexuality Popular and How Do Young People Feel about It?

Hollywood has glamorized the gay lifestyle by its hip stamp of approval and has portrayed homosexual relationships as merely alternative lifestyles. Until recently, TV programs and movies rarely showed homosexuals; today, homosexuality is not only a common occurrence, but presented as normal behavior.

Because of Hollywood's contribution to the gay rights movement, within a few years, debates concerning whether homosexuality is right or wrong will be a non-issue to many in the world and perhaps even to some in the church. Even now, it is very much politically correct to accept homosexual relationships as a non-threatening alternative to traditional heterosexual marriages.

Along these same lines, being gay now appears to be a fad with young people trying it out to see what it's all about. A recent *Seventeen* magazine poll asked the question: "How many teens are okay with homosexuality?" In 1991, only 17 percent said they were okay with it; by 1999, that percentage had grown to 54 percent.

Of course, teens saying they're "okay with it" doesn't by any stretch of the imagination mean they're all experimenting with it, but it does strongly imply that attitudes are changing, especially among young people, as we slowly become more tolerant.

The Homosexual Mindset

Many homosexuals believe they were born gay. They claim there was never a time in their lives when they were not attracted to the same sex. Why, they ask, would anyone choose to be gay? It is not an easy life to live. Even though homosexual conduct is more accepted today than in the past, people for the most part are still not accepting. Some are judgmental and many are uncaring. Why would anyone choose to be this way?—or so goes the argument.

The controversial theory that one is born homosexual has been debated for years. Even those in the scientific community who have conducted studies about whether one inherits homosexual tendencies or if environmental conditions are responsible are divided in their opinions and admit that their findings are inconclusive at best.

In his book, *God at a Distance*, Kerry Duke addresses human choice, environment, and heredity in homosexuality:

> Human choice in sexual orientation does not deny that some individuals may have certain inclinations because of peculiar traits in bodily composition. We are born with physical weakness as well as physical strengths and some of these inherited characteristics influence our actions. For instance, some are born with a low ability to cope with the effects of alcohol and have a greater tendency toward alcoholism . . . In the same way, certain genetic and hormonal peculiarities may cause some to be prone to feelings of attraction toward those of the same sex. The feelings themselves may be involuntary and spontaneous. But to experience a feeling is one thing; how one responds to it is a different matter. Those who have an attraction toward the same sex also have the capability to control this feeling . . . Neither biological preconditions nor damaging childhood experiences force one to be a homosexual. Overcoming these sexual obstacles is very difficult, but they can be conquered just as other seemingly insuperable contrary forces in life may be.

These issues will undoubtedly continue to be debated in the future, but they are beyond the scope of this book. Biblically speaking, Christian young women need to understand the bottom line in dealing with homosexual behavior—and that is, God disapproves of it and condemns it in the Scriptures. This doesn't mean God doesn't love those who are living in homosexual relationships, but He does not approve of that behavior.

We know from studying the Bible that God did not create man to be homosexual. He made each of us in His own image: "So God created man in His own image; in the image of God He created him; male and female He created them" (Genesis 1:27).

From creation God obviously made a distinction between man and woman. He created us uniquely as male and female and perfectly suitable for each other. Homosexuality goes against God's original design for man, woman, and marriage. Speaking of the first marriage, Jesus told the Pharisees:

> He who made them at the beginning "made them male and female," and said, "For this reason a man shall leave his father and mother and be joined to his wife, and the two shall become one flesh." So then, they are no longer two but one flesh. Therefore what God has joined together, let not man separate" (Matthew 19:4-6).

Another example of the incredible way God made each of us is found in Psalms 139:13–14. David said: "For You formed my inward parts; You covered me in my mother's womb. I will praise You, for I am fearfully and wonderfully made." What powerful words and what an awesome thought—each of us is made in the image of God and in such a wonderful way!

A fence-straddling attitude that tolerates unrepentant homosexual activity will damage the church and the name of Christ. We as Christians must display a loving, yet non-compromising, attitude toward those living in homosexuality.

The good news that has come about lately amidst all the problems in the homosexual world is that some are now leaving that lifestyle. Some Christians are now actively helping those who desire to get out of homosexuality. With the Bible as our guide, we can be assured God always stands willing to forgive those who repent and turn from their sinful lifestyles.

What Does the Bible Say about Homosexuality?

Some gay relationships appear normal and stable; it seems that no one is actually hurting anyone. Why would society and the church look down on homosexuals? What's so wrong with being gay? Does the Bible say anything about it? Yes, it does, contrary to what the world says about it.

Although Jesus never mentioned or condemned homosexuality, per se, during His ministry, He did strongly condemn sexual immorality—specifically adultery and fornication. But in condemning sexual immorality, He condemned homosexual relationships. Second Timothy 3:16 teaches us that the entire Bible is inspired of God, so we must have a healthy respect for all Scripture. Three of those scriptures, written by inspiration of God from the pen of the apostle Paul, that strongly and plainly condemn homosexual behavior are discussed below:

- *Galatians 5:19–21*

  Now the works of the flesh are evident, which are: adultery, fornication, uncleanness, lewdness, idolatry, sorcery, hatred, contentions, jealousies, outbursts of wrath, selfish ambitions, dissensions, heresies, envy, murders, drunkenness, revelries, and the like; of which I tell you beforehand, just as I also told you in time past, that those who practice such things will not inherit the kingdom of God.

  In this passage, Paul wrote these plain words condemning the "works of the flesh"—and what a range of sins he covered! The so-called soft sins, such as jealousy, envy, and selfish ambition, are listed alongside the "biggies"—murder, adultery, fornication, and uncleanness.

  Here, *uncleanness* refers to moral impurity and sexual immorality. Although homosexuality is not specifically listed, it easily falls into that uncleanness category. Anyone trying to justify homosexuality because it is not specifically mentioned in this passage presents a weak argument, seeing that Paul also said anyone who participated in the activities specifically condemned, or any like them, would not inherit the kingdom of God.

- *Romans 1:26–27*

  For this reason, God gave them up to vile passions. For even their women exchanged the natural use for what is against nature. Likewise also the men, leaving the natural use of the woman, burned in their lust for one another, men with men committing what is shameful, and receiving in themselves the penalty of their error which was due.

Homosexuality was widespread in Paul's day as it is in ours today. God allowed people then—and He allows us today—to have choice, and He doesn't step in to keep us from making our individual choices. In this passage, Paul writes about the unnatural passions and homosexual acts of some in that day. He spoke about Gentiles who went against nature by engaging in same-sex relations. This passage is significant because it teaches that even those without knowledge of the Scriptures know that homosexual behavior is wrong, since nature itself declares it to be immoral. Although Paul goes on to mention many other sins in verses 29 through 31, he concludes by saying that God's decree in the matter is that those who commit those sins deserve death—and not only those who continue to practice those sins, but also those who approve of the activity. Very strong words, indeed!

- *1 Corinthians 6:9–11*

  Do you not know that the unrighteous will not inherit the kingdom of God? Do not be deceived. Neither fornicators, nor idolaters, nor adulterers, nor homosexuals, nor sodomites, nor thieves, nor covetous, nor drunkards, nor revilers, nor extortionists will inherit the kingdom of God. And such were some of you. But you were washed, but you were sanctified, but you were justified in the name of the Lord Jesus and by the Spirit of our God.

The city of Corinth and the church there struggled with every imaginable sin. Paul lists many sins in this passage, saying we should not be deceived, that those who continue to practice those sins will not inherit the kingdom of God.

He wasn't saying in this passage that adulterers, drunkards, or homosexuals are automatically excluded from going to Heaven. In verse 11 he goes on to say "and such were some of you," meaning that some of the Christians in Corinth had once been homosexuals, drunkards, thieves, and so on. We see that after these Corinthians became Christians, they stopped their sinful practices, including homosexuality. If homosexuality were not a choice, would it not have been impossible for those individuals to change their behavior? They had been cleansed, though, by the blood of Christ and thus stopped their sinful practices.

It is the message we need to remember today. No matter what the sin, Christ changes people, and we can be forgiven.

Carrie's Story

If you think that homosexuality does not exist in the church, think again. As a Bible teacher, I have met and talked with students and counselors who have, many times over, confirmed that dreaded truth. Meet a homosexual church member now.

Carrie became a Christian as a young lady, and she and her family were active in the church. Her father was an elder. In spite of her strong Christian background, Carrie became sexually involved with another woman after her marriage failed.

When asked how she became involved in homosexuality, Carrie replied, "I don't know how it happened. My first lesbian relationship started out as a friendship with another woman that grew over time, and before I knew what happened, I had begun an emotional, then a physical relationship with her."

Carrie continued, "I had passing thoughts of being with a woman before, but I never thought I would actually act on those feelings. Once I did, though, I felt hooked. I thought this might just be experimental or something I would grow out of, but it took hold of me and held me in its grip for years."

Although each affair she entered was initially promising, Carrie endured years of one failed relationship after another with women. She found no stability, little acceptance or support from others, extreme personal guilt, and no future in it.

Carrie also admitted, "Since I had been raised to know right from wrong, I knew that homosexuality was wrong, but I was determined to be the best lesbian I could be! How could God disapprove of me if I was a good person, committed to my relationship, and with a consenting adult? I wasn't hurting anyone."

Over the years, Carrie attempted to hang on to some semblance of Christianity because of her upbringing, yet she remained in lesbian relationships. She expressed her guilt, shame, confusion, and hopelessness and told of the double life she endured.

She said, "Many of my friends who were in the same predicament turned to alcohol and drugs, as I did, to escape the guilt and shame we felt. Some became so despondent they considered suicide." Carrie's attempts to live for Christ while continuing to live in homosexuality didn't work, and the lifestyle eventually wore her down.

The Christian's Attitude toward Homosexuality

How should we as Christians view homosexuality? How do we deal with people such as Carrie or young Nicole? Can we be compassionate to those who are practicing homosexuality without compromising the truth? Consider the following ways we can approach this subject:

- *Get Off the Fence and Take a Stand against It.* Homosexuality is sinful. Christians must never lose sight of this, regardless of personal opinions, or how strong the gay rights movement becomes, or whether or not we have homosexual friends. We must have the courage to teach what the Bible says about homosexuality without compromising. To be effective, it must be done in love.

- *Don't Be Homophobic.* Christians should never belittle or make fun of those practicing homosexuality. Rather, we should be kind, compassionate, and loving toward them. Homosexuals should not be feared, hated, or ridiculed by Christians, but taught in love about the forgiveness, peace, and salvation that is offered by being in Christ. There is no place in the church for homophobia any more than there is a place for racism.

- *Be Compassionate to Homosexuals Who Are Seeking the Truth.* Should we accept them in our worship services? Yes—just as we would accept an alcoholic or other individual who might be struggling with various moral or spiritual problems. This is not to say we should continue to accept and fellowship homosexuals who blatantly refuse to repent of their behavior. In his tract, "Works of the Flesh: Homosexuality," Tom Holland explains this masterfully:

> The church of Christ will accept into fellowship people who have been involved in various kinds of sin such as drunkenness, adultery, or homosexuality. However, these people must have a penitent heart and receive pardon from the Lord. If a drunkard repents, he stops drinking alcohol. If an adulterer repents, he ceases to commit adultery. If a homosexual repents, he/she no longer commits homosexual acts . . . God's Word instructs penitent people to be baptized for the remission of sins (Acts 2:38). Those penitent people who are baptized but then live again in sin, such as homosexuality, are directed by God's Word to repent and pray for forgiveness (Acts 8:22; 8:12–13).

- *Be a Shining Example of the Love Shown By Jesus Christ.* We might be the only link the homosexual has to the love and forgiveness of Jesus. We must show them the love that Jesus exhibited to all with whom He came in contact.

- *Be Willing to Reach Out and Touch the Untouchable.* Jesus was known for His association with sinners and those who were considered losers. His love for all people was amazing then and today! We, as Christians, must learn to have that same spirit of love and be willing to help anyone who is in need. We must never think ourselves to be too good to help those who are hurting, such as those individuals with AIDS, or those desiring to get out of homosexuality.

Tips for Overcoming Homosexuality

For most young Christian women, homosexuality will never be an issue. It can happen, though, as evidenced by Carrie's story. What do you do if you or someone you love does become trapped in homosexuality? The following suggestions are offered to help anyone who may be a slave to this sinful and destructive behavior:

- *Realize It Is Possible to Get Out.* Getting out of the homosexual lifestyle is often very hard, especially for those who have been involved in gay relationships for years. There are examples after examples, however, of those who are doing just that today. Some have married and have families; others remain celibate. Many tell of the relief and peace they are now experiencing since leaving their homosexual lifestyles.

  The gay activists don't want these stories publicized, because it negates their theory that one is born homosexual and can't change. Romans 8:31 says, "If God is for us, who can be against us?" Those are encouraging words for anyone trying to leave the homosexual lifestyle.

- *Repent and Stop the Homosexual Activity.* The Bible teaches us that God condemns homosexual acts. Even though some may be tempted by homosexuality, nothing says they have to fulfill every desire. Homosexuality may always be a temptation to some, but the sexual activity must be stopped to be pleasing to God. This may require leading a celibate lifestyle.

- *Realize God Will Provide a Way of Escape.* Jesus Christ prom-ised that He will not allow anyone to be tempted with more than they can bear. Even if the situation seems hopeless, God has promised to deliver. For those individuals sincerely desir-ing to come out of homosexuality, there is no more encourag-ing verse in the Bible than 1 Corinthians 10:13:

  > No temptation has overtaken you except such as is common to man; but God is faithful, who will not allow you to be tempted beyond what you are able, but with the temptation will also make the way of escape, that you may be able to bear it.

- *Have Faith in God and Pray for Strength.* Philippians 4:13 says, "I can do all things through Christ who strengthens me."

- *Associate with Christian Friends.* Persons coming out of homo-sexuality must have some other form of affection and friend-ship offered to them. Something positive must be offered in its place. Hopefully, Christians will see this need and provide friendship to the person desiring to leave the homosexual lifestyle.

- *Let Go of Opinions.* Realize that opinions do not count for much in deciding whether homosexuality, or any other activity, is right or wrong. God has made it plain in His Word that homo-sexuality is wrong, and we must respect that and accept it, regardless of our opinions.

- *Seek Good, Competent Christian Counseling.* It is important to seek compassionate and competent Christian counseling. While it may be necessary in some instances to seek therapy or psychological help, remember that some secular psychol-ogy promotes the notion that homosexuality cannot be over-come.

Hope in Christ

Carrie's story had a happy ending. After many years of living in one failed gay relationship after another, the fence straddling finally wore Carrie down. After carefully reviewing the Scriptures, diligently studying them, and understanding what the inspired writers of the Bible taught about homosexuality, she stopped her homosexual behavior and turned her life back over to God.

She said, "I was never truly happy or satisfied while living in lesbian relationships because of the way I had been raised, and neither was I happy in my pitiful attempt to still be a Christian. The heavy burden of guilt never left me during all those years."

Today, Carrie has returned to the church, is living a celibate lifestyle, and has many new friends. She is a new creature in Christ and is no longer enslaved to a lifestyle that promises so much, but delivers so little.

It's Your Turn!

1. Is being gay a sin? Give scripture to support your answer.

2. Why is there so much hatred, prejudice, and ridicule shown toward homosexuals? How should we as Christians react when fellow Christians demonstrate the same hatred, prejudice, and ridicule?

3. Discuss the problem of homosexuality in the church and in schools. Do most young people accept homosexuality as an alternate lifestyle?

4. How should parents react if they discover their child is practicing homosexuality?

5. Why do you think God condemns homosexuality—especially if it does not seem to be hurting anyone or anything? Is God cruel to condemn homosexuals who have sincerely tried to "go straight"? Explain your answer.

6. What rights should homosexuals have in the work place? How should homosexuals be treated when they attend a place of worship?

7. Is gay rights a civil right's issue or a moral issue? Why?

8. Discuss AIDS as God's punishment for homosexuals.

9. How should the church handle openly gay members? Should they be fellowshipped?

10. Is homosexuality something a person is, like skin color, elderly, female, or handicapped; or is it something one does, like adultery or incest? Discuss your conclusions.

CHAPTER SEVEN

Marriage: I Do!

Compromising Our Standards

Fence-Straddling Position: "We can always get a divorce if this doesn't work out."

Bible Position: "Marriage is honorable among all, and the bed undefiled, but fornicators and adulterers God will judge" (Hebrews 13:4).

Scripture Search

Genesis 2:18–25   Ephesians 5:21–32
Proverbs 5:15–20   Colossians 3:18–21
Ecclesiastes 9:9   1 Peter 3:7
Hebrews 13:4   1 Corinthians 7:1–6
2 Timothy 2:22

Say What?

Standards—Morals, ethics, and habits that are considered acceptable by authority, custom, or an individual.

Submit—To give over or yield to the authority of another. Compliant; humbly obedient.

Spouse—Husband or wife.

Lasciviousness—Lustful; lewd. Arousing or inciting sexual desire.

Lust—Sexual desire or appetite, especially when uncontrolled or illicit.

Promiscuous—Engaging in sexual relations indiscriminately or with many persons.

Cohabitation—Living together without being married.

Monogamous—The practice of marrying only once in life. Having only one mate.

Adultery—Sexual relations between a married person and someone other than his or her spouse.

Fornication—Sexual immorality.

Yes!

Gregg had finally popped the question. After a year of dating, Cindy and Gregg were engaged.

"Morgan!" Cindy practically shouted into the phone to her best friend. "Guess what. I'm getting married!"

"Hey, that's great. I am so excited for you—when's the big day?" Morgan asked.

"We haven't set the date yet." Cindy couldn't stop talking. "Gregg will graduate from the community college next month, and he's already started an exciting job with the new technology center. I've decided to drop out of college for a while, since I've just taken a promising job with a sales company. Both our jobs require us to travel a lot, so we are really excited about seeing the world and— oh, everything just seems to be going great! I can hardly wait to

start planning the wedding. It will probably be sometime this spring."

"Are you still planning on a big church wedding?"

"Oh, yes—I wouldn't miss that for the world! Mom has already started talking about the showers, the parties, the reception, my gown. There is so much to think about! Can you believe it? My parents have actually agreed to hire a wedding planner—just to make sure everything goes well. After all, this is a once-in-a-lifetime event, and we want to make sure everything is perfect for our wedding."

As Cindy continued talking, Morgan suddenly remembered that Gregg was not a Christian. In spite of Cindy's exciting news, Morgan could not seem to shake that thought. "Cindy, did Gregg ever become a Christian?"

"Well, no, why in the world would you ask that now?" Cindy's voice quieted and the pitch lowered. "Actually, he doesn't go to church anywhere right now, but he is a good person."

Morgan didn't respond.

Cindy began to feel her face flush, and she couldn't keep the bitter words from her lips. "Morgan, can't you ever be happy for anyone? This is one of the happiest days of my life and now you've ruined it by implying Gregg is just not good enough! You worry too much—about everything. Gregg's a wonderful man—everything will turn out fine, you just wait and see . . ."

In spite of turbulent times and soaring divorce rates, most women today still hope to marry, establish families, and build homes. The staggering number of divorces granted each year indicates that marriage relationships can indeed be fragile, but many couples today are successfully building happy and lasting marriages. Some experts say it is a myth that marriages are automatically destined to fail. In the United States, 61 percent of people are married, 23 percent have never been married, 8 percent are widowed, and only 8 percent are divorced. That doesn't mean marriage is easy! Having a successful marriage means we must invest our whole being into making it work.

Today marriage is not given the thought and prayerful planning it deserves, and many times young people don't respect it enough. Often more thought is given to planning the bridal shower, wedding ceremony, and honeymoon than to the actual serious business of marriage itself.

Reading a recent email, I was reminded of how much society as a whole has belittled marriage and how much we have compromised our standards. Among a list of new terms in this email was this one: *"Starter Marriage:* A first marriage that ends in divorce, with no kids, no property, and no regrets." What a pity! Truly, how we have cheapened marriage.

Why Marry Anyway?

Is it possible for a young Christian woman to have a happy marriage? Of course it is! God instituted marriage in the Garden of Eden, and it pleases Him very much for a man and woman to marry. Why do people marry anyway? Many good reasons come to mind, but let's look at four below:

1. *For Sexual Fulfillment and to Avoid Fornication.* Sexual intimacy is the special relationship by which a man and a woman express their love to each other, both physically and emotionally. Our physical sexual desires are natural and God-given, and God designed marriage as a way to satisfy these desires and to help men and women guard against sexual temptation. Since God created sex, He meant for it to be a beautiful experience within marriage, certainly not something shameful or embarrassing.

   In 2 Timothy 2:22, Paul admonishes Timothy, a young man, to "flee also youthful lusts." We are to run from those things that tempt us sexually. Only in marriage should the sexual desires God has given to everyone be fulfilled completely. The Song of Solomon and many beautiful proverbs speak of the joy and pleasure of enjoying our spouses sexually.

   In 1 Corinthians 7:3–5, Paul taught that married couples have a responsibility to care for each other sexually, so husbands and wives should not withhold themselves physically from one another, but should fulfill each other's needs and desires. A young woman and man contemplating marriage must understand marriage is God's plan for sexual fulfillment and must be willing to forsake all others and remain faithful and loving to each other for life.

2. *For Companionship.* In the beginning, God saw that it was "not good that man should be alone," thus God created woman for the man as a perfect helpmate. It is human nature for us to desire companionship. In marriage, being good friends to each other is as important as being faithful sexual partners. The companionship found in marriage provides an avenue for communication and a partner to share the general day-to-day, year-to-year activities that make up life. Sharing interests, establishing traditions, and making memories with our mates constitute true companionship.

3. *To Establish an Earthly Symbol of Christ and His Bride, the Church.* In Ephesians 5:25–27, Paul gives a very high view of marriage and compares it to the relationship between Christ and the church. Husbands are told to love their wives as Christ loved the church and gave Himself for it. A husband should also love his wife as he loves his own body, feeding it and taking care of it. Women were instructed in verse 33 to respect their husbands and in verse 22 to yield to them. Why? Because the husband is the head of the wife, just as Christ is the head of the church. Someone has to be in charge of the marriage, and God delegated that responsibility and privilege to the man.

Submitting to our husbands doesn't mean he is more important than we are. Being the head of the wife and family is his role, just as the wife's role is to be submissive, to be the homemaker, and to manage the home. It doesn't mean the woman is inferior to the man or that the husband should rule over her harshly. The wife certainly shouldn't become a doormat, but she should acknowledge her husband's leadership. Our perfect example, Christ, showed humility and submitted to His father, and wives should also submit to their husbands.

In a marriage relationship, God actually wants both the husband and wife to be submissive. For the wife, this means willingly following her husband's leadership in Christ. For the husband, it means putting aside his own interests in order to care for his wife.

Submission is rarely a problem in homes where both partners have a strong relationship with Christ and where each is concerned for the happiness of the other. As a young woman, it is important that you choose a husband who will treat you as tenderly and lovingly as Christ does the church, and one to whom you are willing and able to submit.

4. *To Establish Families and Build Homes.* God intended that marriage would be the institution whereby homes would be established and children born and raised by a mother and a father. Children are truly a gift from the Lord and should be cherished (Psalms 127:3). In 1 Timothy 5:14, the younger women were encouraged to marry, have children, and manage their homes.

How To Be Assured of a Happy Marriage

Smart dating provides the basis for a strong and happy marriage. We should not straddle the fence or compromise our standards when choosing a man with the important characteristics and traits desired in a husband. We should be careful about blindly falling in love and being overwhelmed by emotionalism, infatuation, and physical attraction.

In the book *Twelve Things I Want My Kids to Remember Forever,* the author made some interesting points concerning that:

> I wasn't about to marry someone with whom I was hopelessly in love, because that's not a good basis for marriage. True love, pure love, unconditional love is not something you fall into. Love is an act of the will. Love is as love does. Love is not a state of being. It's an action verb, an act of will. Love is doing.

With that in mind, consider the following suggestions on how to best choose a husband. Choose a man who is:

• *A Christian.* Choose a faithful Christian man. There is no specific commandment in the Bible that a person must marry a Christian, but it will definitely make your life easier. In 2 Corinthians 6:14, Paul forbade Christians to be unequally yoked with unbelievers. There are dangers when believers are yoked together with unbelievers, since they are ultimately headed in opposite directions, and their interests or priorities in life may not be the same.

It is not unscriptural to be married to an unbeliever, though, since in 1 Corinthians 7:12–13, Paul told those Christians to stay with their unbelieving spouses if at all possible. Some very fine marriages are the result of the Christian partner winning the unbeliever to Christ after they married, but the opposite is true more times than not. Often, it is the Christian who is brought down. It may not seem a big deal when dating, but this area can eventually turn into a point of contention. Date only Christians and choose a good, faithful Christian man for a husband.

- *Committed.* Choose a man who is committed first to God. Then, make sure he is committed to the marriage vows, the happiness of his family, and the church. Make a commitment to stick it out. Don't quit when the times get tough, since things usually have a way of getting better over time.

- *Caring and Kind.* These basic characteristics, hopefully learned at an early age, are important to any marriage. Choose someone who is easy to get along with and is capable of sharing and enjoying the simple things in life. A sense of humor goes a long way too! Verse 4 of 1 Corinthians 13, the Bible's love chapter, simply says, "Love is patient, love is kind."

- *Complimentary.* Why choose a man who never builds up anyone, is full of put-downs, and never has a complimentary thing to say? Choose a man who is uplifting, encouraging, and complimentary. This little trait can go a long way in assuring a happy marriage.

- *Communicative.* Nothing is more frustrating and destructive than being in a marriage where there is no communication. Choose a man who will talk, listen, and communicate. Lack of communication is a sure way of assuring an unhappy marriage.

- *Compatible.* Choose a mate who is compatible and will be a good, faithful companion over the years. Having different interests as well as similar likes and dislikes can also be important.

Who's Marrying Today?

Not every woman will or should marry. Although Proverbs 18:22 says, "He who finds a wife finds a good thing, and obtains favor from the Lord," there is no commandment in the Bible that every person should marry. Paul devoted an entire chapter to this in 1 Corinthians 7, saying that it would probably be better to be as he was—not married. First Corinthians 7:34 says:

> The unmarried woman cares about the things of the Lord, that she may be holy both in body and in spirit. But she who is married cares about the things of the world—how she may please her husband.

Some women today are choosing to remain single, although it's doubtful their reasons are always as noble as staying single to work for the Lord. Sometimes it's selfishness, but there's nothing inherently wrong with remaining single. Many women have excellent jobs and are no longer financially dependent on a husband; some say they are happier alone. Statistics show, however, that married people generally report greater happiness. Single life can get lonely at times and the responsibilities overwhelming. Not everyone is cut out for the single life.

Being single often means having less joy (no one to share your happiness); it creates additional labor (no one to share the load); and there is more grief and sadness (no one to share the emotion). It can also be financially and emotionally overwhelming (no one to offer encouragement or assistance); it renders achievement less rewarding (no one to applaud); and it is sometimes socially unacceptable (try going to a party without a mate).

A single woman must be extremely strong in several other areas too—morally, to withstand physical desires and sexual temptation; emotionally, when there is no one to lean on; financially, to support herself; socially, to be able to intermingle with others; and spiritually, to remain faithful to God when it often seems no one really cares.

Fewer American women are marrying today and many are marrying later in life. In 1970, the average age for women and men to marry was 21 and 23, respectively; in 1998, that age had risen to 25 for women and 27 for men. One reason for that, however, could be the trend over the past few years for couples to live together without the benefit of marriage, either as a trial period before marriage or as a permanent situation.

Cohabitation

When Will asked Elizabeth to move in with him, she could hardly contain her excitement! They had been dating for nearly a year and their relationship was on the fast track toward marriage.

Elizabeth said, "Will was the most exciting man I'd ever met, and just the fact he wanted me to be close to him before our marriage only made things better. We discussed it thoroughly and felt it was in our best interest to move in together and share an apartment."

From a practical standpoint, Will was also quick to point out they would save money by having only one residence, they could get to know each other better, and plan for their upcoming wedding.

Five years later, they still were not married, and Will made the painful decision to tell Elizabeth he was having second thoughts about marriage after all: "I think it would be best if we separated for a while. I need some space to make sure this is what I really want in life."

In 1999, five million couples in the United States lived together without being married, and in 2000, the number of unmarried-partner households shot up 72 percent nationwide. Though the practice of living together prior to marriage was totally unacceptable just a few years ago, it has lost much of its stigma in the past few years.

In 1996, an NBC News poll discovered that 66 percent of young people ages 18 to 32 believe a couple should first live together before they get married. Forty-five percent of all women in the United States between the ages of 25 and 34 have at one time lived with someone.

Why do so many choose to live together before marrying? Many give a financial reason as Will did. Why should they pay for two households when they could live together cheaper? Some fear divorce and its consequences, so they decide to try things out first and then decide about marriage. Some want to see if they are compatible sexually. Many think this trial period will assure them of a happier marriage.

Statistics do not show this to be true. Only one couple in five who cohabit ever marry each other. A December 1996 issue of the *Houston Chronicle* reported couples that live together have an 80 percent greater chance of getting a divorce than those who don't. Those living together prior to marriage are more likely to divorce than those who do not. Practice does not make perfect!

What does God have to say about all this? It is plain in His Word that this type behavior is not acceptable at all; God condemns fornication. First Corinthians 6:9–10; Galatians 5:19–21; 1 Timothy 1:9–10; and other scriptures plainly state that fornicators will not inherit the kingdom of God.

Christian women should avoid cohabitation at all cost. In addition to being unacceptable in God's sight, women who live with their boyfriends nearly always get the short end of the deal. The man usually has little to lose. He gets a partner for companionship and free sex, yet he can pack his bags and leave at any time, since there is no real commitment involved.

In one survey of over a hundred couples that lived together, 71 percent of the women said they would not live-in again. Cohabitation is all about the moment, while marriage should be "until death do us part." Think about it!

The Two-Year Commitment

In their book, *The Ten Commandments of Dating,* Ben Young and Dr. Samuel Adams present an interesting concept called "the two-year commitment." It means that no matter how great it feels to be around a particular person and no matter how fast the hormones are pumping, the couple will invest two years of their life in getting to know the other person before committing to marriage. It doesn't mean they enter into a two-year cohabitation with that person or into a long-term relationship with everyone they date, but when they believe they have found the right person, they allow at least two years from the first date to the wedding date.

Many times we let our hearts, rather than our heads, lead us into marriage, resulting in disastrous consequences. Women often seem to enjoy a challenge, too, thinking we can change his little idiosyncrasies and annoying habits after we get married. Usually, though, what we see is what we get!

If your boyfriend doesn't go to church with you before you marry, he probably won't go after the wedding, either. If he drinks and is abusive or is not a good communicator while dating, will he suddenly become a different person after you're married? It usually just does not turn out that way. The idea of the two-year commitment plan is to give a couple plenty of time to get to know one another. Then they will not rush into marriage based on infatuation and physical attraction alone. Young and Adams report that many singles are uncomfortable about the idea of committing to a two-year period, but it does give the couple a great opportunity to make sure they are choosing the right person.

Ten Questions to Ask before Walking Down the Aisle

Marriage ranks as one of the most important decisions you as a young Christian woman will ever make. To assure that your marriage will be truly happy, it's good to address any critical questions or issues before the big day arrives. If you're contemplating marriage, ask yourself these ten questions.

1. *Are You Both Christians?* This is probably the most important question you can ask yourself. Since you will eventually marry someone you date, date only faithful Christian men. Marrying a faithful Christian is a decision you won't regret. Also, be willing to look at yourself in the mirror and make sure you're the person you need to be.

2. *Are You Old Enough to Marry?* Are you mature enough to marry at 17, 18, and 19 years of age—or even at 25? Have you had time to determine in your mind what you want in a marriage?

3. *Do You Trust Each Other to Remain Faithful to the Marriage Vows?* Once trust is destroyed, either by sexual unfaithfulness or indifference to the marriage itself, it is virtually impossible to re-establish.

4. *Are You Sexually Attracted to Each Other and Do You Genuinely Like Each Other?* These may appear to be silly questions, but both are important. The right chemistry is very important; don't ignore it if it isn't there. To be successful, a good marriage also needs true friendship and companionship, as well as sexual attraction.

5. *What Is Your Financial Situation?* Do both of you have a good understanding of the cost of maintaining a marriage? How well do both of you handle money? Are you financially able to marry? Do either or both of you have a job or a promise of one?

6. *Will Both of You Work outside the Home?* Has a mutual understanding been reached concerning having two careers? Who

will be responsible for the household chores and keeping the children if your job requires that you travel?

7. *Do You Both Want to Have Children?* Do you both like children? Will you work after having children or will you stay at home? Would you be agreeable to adopting a child if you cannot have one?

8. *Are You Willing to Accept Change?* You and your husband won't always be the same. Over time, you may have to accept job changes, health concerns, financial hardships, children challenges, and the realization that your bodies and minds will change as you age.

9. *Are You Willing to Submit to Your Husband?* As unpopular as the concept of submission is today, the Bible states that the wife is to submit to her husband (Ephesians 5:22). If you aren't willing to do this, perhaps you shouldn't marry at all.

10. *Are You Totally Committed to the Marriage?* Do you have a deep love and affection for your fiancé and are you both totally committed to do everything within your power to make the marriage successful and happy?

If you feel good about your answers to the above questions, you are well on your way to understanding and appreciating the awesome responsibility and privilege of marriage. Pray to God for guidance and wisdom in choosing your mate for life. It can be a wonderful adventure!

It's Your Turn!

1. What are some reasons for marrying? For not marrying?

2. What is your personal opinion of the ideal age to marry? How do you know when you are ready to marry?

3. What does the Bible teach about a couple living together before marriage?

4. How do you feel about the two-year commitment presented in this study? What are its good points and bad points?

5. What are some advantages of married life?

6. Do you think everyone should marry? What are the advantages and disadvantages of remaining single?

7. What does it mean to submit to your husband?

8. Discuss society's double standards for men and women concerning sex before marriage. Why is it so?

9. How do you determine your sexual limits when dating?

10. Are you planning to marry a Christian? What are the disadvantages of marrying one who is not a Christian?

CHAPTER EIGHT

We're Getting a Divorce

Compromising Our Commitment

Fence-Straddling Position: "My marriage just didn't work out, so I'm getting a divorce. It's time to move on and live my life. I'm getting married again—I deserve some happiness."

Bible Position: "And I say to you, whoever divorces his wife, except for sexual immorality, and marries another, commits adultery; and whoever marries her who is divorced commits adultery" (Matthew 19:9).

Scripture Search

Deuteronomy 24:1–4   Mark 10:2–12
Malachi 2:14–16   Luke 16:18
Matthew 5:32   Romans 7:1–4
Matthew 19:3–9   1 Corinthians 7:10–16
Ephesians 5:31

Say What?

Commitment—A pledge; an agreement to do something. Obligated; driven forward by a strong moral pressure.

Adultery—Sexual relations between a married person and someone other than his or her spouse.

Fornication—Sexual immorality.

Infidelity—Marital unfaithfulness.

Incompatibility—Incapable of existing together in harmony.

Abusive—Treating someone in a harmful, injurious, or offensive way or speaking to someone in an insulting, belittling, or harsh manner.

Affair—A romantic or passionate attachment to someone, usually of a short duration.

Cleave—Cling; stick together closely; to remain faithful.

Spouse—Husband or wife.

Submit—Compliant, humbly obedient. To give over or yield to the authority of another.

"Cindy!" shouted Morgan, "It's so good to see you again! I haven't seen you since your wedding—nearly two years now. How's everything?"

"Not bad, I guess," replied Cindy, smiling. "I'm still working at the same job, I've been traveling some, going to night school, and just moved into a new condo."

"That sounds great! How are you and Gregg doing? Are you still attending services at the new congregation you told me about?" asked Morgan.

"Well, no, actually I'm not going to church anywhere right now. It was too much of a hassle to go with all the traveling I was doing, and Gregg never went with me. I know I should be going, but it's hard, you know."

She suddenly stopped. "I guess you haven't heard . . . Gregg and I have been divorced about nine months now," said Cindy quietly.

"Divorced?" asked Morgan, shocked. "You and Gregg? Divorced? Of all people, I can't believe it! You seemed so perfect together. What happened? Don't tell me it was someone else!"

"No, not at all. We both worked crazy schedules; both jobs required a lot of travel. We just drifted apart."

"I really hate to hear that." Morgan paused and then added. "You seem to be handling this pretty well. How's Gregg taking it?"

"Actually, okay, I guess. I heard he's already seeing someone else." Cindy hesitated, then continued excitedly: "And guess what. So am I!"

"Wow, that was fast!" Morgan was genuinely surprised at the change in her old friend. "Is it serious?"

"Well, his name is Dave, and he's been so supportive of me during all this. He's just gone through a divorce too. Same old story— incompatibility. I guess we all married too young. Anyway, I feel really good about this. Who knows—maybe there will be another wedding in the future. You know what they say: Life goes on . . ."

In a perfect world, there is no divorce; everyone indeed lives happily ever after. Unfortunately, our world is not perfect. Although the Bible teaches that death is the only honorable way for a marriage to end, sometimes in spite of all efforts, people do divorce. It has become a sad way of life.

Cindy and Gregg's young marriage ended quickly, with both of them divorced by age 22. After such a promising start, what happened? Why the divorce? Immaturity played a big part. Soon after their marriage, a fierce independent streak kicked in and Cindy decided she just didn't want to be married any more. Her new job quickly turned into a solid career path for her, and she began college classes two nights a week.

Gregg, busy with his stressful new job, traveled weeks on end for most of the short marriage. The adage, "absence makes the heart grow fonder," proved false. Distance stressed their fragile relationship, and it began to unravel right away.

Selfishly choosing her education and career, Cindy quickly adapted to a new lifestyle of happy hours, job-related activities, and new friends. It seemed as though she saw less and less of Gregg. In all honesty, Cindy began to enjoy her newly found freedom and independence. Why didn't she realize prior to marriage that she wanted to be footloose and fancy-free?

Their no-fault divorce took only a few minutes. Cindy felt strange signing a few papers and then just walking away, free again—or so she thought. Though she tried to ignore it, something inside her seemed to say, "This may not be so easy after all." After the dust settled, Cindy knew she had made a decision that would radically affect the course of her life.

Though they both moved on and began "getting on with their lives," Cindy still can't quite shake wondering what might have been. She still thinks of Gregg from time to time and wonders how his life will turn out. What would their lives together have been like if they had remained married? Would they have had children? What kind of family could they have built?

The Reality of Divorce

Many young people, some with strong Christian backgrounds and good parental examples, are not trained for marriage. And even at the supposedly mature age of twenty, immaturity often wins over reason. Instead of marriage being a lifetime commitment as God planned, it often becomes a dismal failure. A new marriage is fragile and is successful only when both partners work hard to make it so.

While Cindy and Gregg's divorce was painful, it was not as painful as most divorces are. Cindy and Gregg had no children, therefore, no decisions to make about visitation privileges or custody rights. They had no house or big possessions to divide. Division of common property—car, house, bank accounts, and the like— is no easy task in most divorce settlements. Cindy was also fortunate in another aspect in that she had a good job and her financial situation did not leave her in poverty.

After the emotional, physical, and spiritual devastation of divorce, each breakup takes on a life of its own. Extended families split by taking sides. If the divorce occurs because of marital infidelity or an affair, the gut-wrenching sense of betrayal may be too much for a person to ever overcome.

If children are involved, things only get worse. Visitation privileges and custody rights weigh heavily on the mind of any parent. The court-mandated, parent-children rules are sometimes more than a parent can bear. One or both parents may also slide into poverty, with one of them—usually the woman—often appealing to the State for assistance.

Does Divorce Really Affect Children?

Yes, children are always negatively affected by divorce. Those who argue that children, because of their innocence and immaturity, are not so affected are only trying to fool themselves. Children often blame themselves for the divorce. Their self-worth is attacked, and many feel unworthy and abandoned. Many children of divorce suffer from depression, thus skewing their social lives and paralyzing academic performance.

During the '70s, when divorce rates began skyrocketing, the prevailing thought regarding divorce was that it wasn't that big a deal for the kids. They would be sad for a while and then get over it. A controversial new book authored by therapist Judith Wallerstein, entitled *The Unexpected Legacy of Divorce,* addresses that point.

Ms. Wallerstein presents her lifetime work from the past three decades in which she examined the lives of 131 children of divorce and how the after-effects impacted the course of their lives. She found that children, at best, take a very long time to get over divorce. Some never do. According to her research, the most profound and harmful effect showed up when the children reached maturity and tried to form their own adult relationships. Many, attempting to find perfect mates, married later in life; yet, they divorced more often than those who did not come from broken homes.

After evaluating the results of her studies, Ms. Wallerstein concluded that a lousy marriage, at least where a child's welfare is concerned, beats a great divorce. Though controversial, her thoughts are certainly worthy of consideration.

What Causes Divorce?

Impulsiveness to marry is cited by many as the number one reason for divorce. Most people do not take time to really get to know the other person before committing to marriage. Physical looks and sexual attraction often get in the way of making a mature decision about whom and when to marry. Other reasons for divorce include:

- *Immaturity.* Some people are just not old enough to accept the many responsibilities of marriage and are not mature enough to stick with it when the going gets tough. Findings based on a 1995 report showed that nearly half of those who marry under age 18, and 40 percent who marry under age 20, will divorce; over age 25, it's just 24 percent. The difference is maturity.

- *Culture of Impatience.* Pamela Paul, author of *The Starter Marriage and the Future of Matrimony,* addresses the cause of high divorce rate among the young this way:

  They are a "one-click culture"—an impatient generation in an impatient society that wants to download life quickly. When the young hit a pothole, they abandon the road. It feels easy to move on, especially if they feel they are nipping something bad in the bud.

- *Financial Problems.* Often, young couples do not take the time to figure how much it will cost to live together. Many times, young people start off well over their heads, opting for an expensive new house, a house full of new furniture, and two new vehicles. Toss in the possibility of a baby on its way— with no budget planning—and they have a sure recipe for disaster.

- *Sexual Problems.* Problems with sexual intimacy often surface when a couple neglects each other's physical needs or ignores them entirely. No marriage is healthy without sexual excitement.

- *Infidelity/Affairs.* These are just modern-day words for fornication, which God condemns in 1 Corinthians 6:9; 1 Timothy 1:9–10; 1 Corinthians 6:18; and other scriptures. The sense of betrayal and the loss of trust that come about when a partner cheats is often—but not always—too big an obstacle to overcome.

- *Lack of Communication and Lack of Commitment.* Lack of communication is a quiet killer of any marriage. It is important that both parties take an active interest in the other's life. Not talking and not listening to each other are stepping-stones to the divorce court. Selfishness causes many individuals to lack the ability to wholly commit to anything or anybody.

- *Alcoholism / Drug Abuse.* Substance abuse causes people to spend money needed for the necessities of life on alcohol and drugs. A home torn apart by alcohol and drug abuse leads families into turmoil, depression, financial bankruptcy, and spiritual ruin.

- *Abuse—Physical and Verbal.* A breakdown in the headship of the home is often evident as some men misuse their strength and power to abuse their wives and children. Constant verbal abuse can be as devastating to one's self-image as physical abuse, though its effects may not always be as easily seen.

- *Incompatibility.* This catch-all term includes any reason a person can think of for getting a divorce. Although silly at first glance, the following tidbits show some frivolous reasons people give for divorcing. The words hit closer to home than many of us would like to admit:

    She married him because he was such a strong, forceful man—
    Then divorced him because he was too dominating.

    He married her because she was so fragile and petite—
    Then divorced her because she was too weak and helpless.

    She married him because he knew how to be a good provider—
    Then divorced him because all he thought about was work.

    He married her because she was steady and sensible—
    Then divorced her because she was boring and dull.

    She married him because he was the life of the party—
    Then divorced him because he wanted to socialize all the time.

    He married her because she was such a good conversationalist—
    Then divorced her because she was too chatty.

How Common Is Divorce?

It's difficult to find an unbiased statistic on the percentages of marriages that end in divorce. A conservative estimate is that at least 40 percent of first marriages end in divorce. Second marriages have an even greater chance of failing, with approximately 60 percent ending in divorce. The chance of divorcing is highest during the third year of marriage.

Regardless of the percentages of marriages that end in divorce, the actual numbers themselves are staggering. One in four Americans have divorced. Over 1.2 million Americans will divorce this year, and more than one million children will be affected. From 1970 to 2000, divorces soared from 4.3 million to 20 million!

How Does God Feel about Divorce?

From the beginning of time, God never planned for man and woman to divorce. He never authorized it, and it was never His intention or desire that anyone would divorce. In Genesis 2:24 these familiar words are spoken: "Therefore a man shall leave his father and mother and be joined to his wife, and they shall become one flesh."

Jesus used those same words in Matthew 19:5 when discussing divorce with the Pharisees. There, the Pharisees had come to trick Jesus, and in verse 3, they asked Him the question, "Is it lawful for a man to divorce his wife for just any reason?" In using those words found in Genesis 2:24, Jesus went back to the beginning of time to get His answer, and He re-emphasized that it was never God's intention that couples divorce.

The Pharisees continued to push Jesus, saying that Moses had allowed a man to write a certificate of divorce and put away his wife (Deuteronomy 24:1–4). Moses had indeed instituted some laws to help its victims. Those civil laws were designed especially to protect the women who, in that culture, were vulnerable when living alone. Those laws made the men think twice before divorcing his wife for any conceivable reason. Jesus said in Matthew 19:8 that the real reason Moses allowed those divorce laws was "because of the hardness of your hearts . . . but from the beginning it was not so."

The most revealing scripture that shows how God really feels about divorce is found in Malachi 2:16: "For the Lord God of Israel says that He hates divorce, for it covers one's garments with violence."

What Does the Bible Say about Divorce and Remarriage?

Too many divorces, often for frivolous reasons, are being granted today. The church should be setting the proper example in our marriages, but in many cases, it isn't. Divorce among Christians is no longer shocking, and remarriage is now a common occurrence. Some statistics show as many as 75 percent of divorced people eventually remarry.

Although it is not a popular topic, and it seems sometimes as though teaching concerning divorce and remarriage has all but stopped in the church, the Bible gives only two reasons to justify remarriage. Those are (1) death of a spouse and (2) divorce resulting from sexual unfaithfulness (fornication).

1. *Death of Spouse.* In 1 Corinthians 7:39, Paul said, "A wife is bound by law as long as her husband lives; but if her husband dies, she is at liberty to be married to whom she wishes, only in the Lord." God intended that marriage be forever and that only death would break that marriage. However, Paul is stating here that a widow may indeed marry "in the Lord."

2. *Divorce Resulting from Sexual Unfaithfulness.* Jesus taught in Matthew 5:32; Matthew 19:9; Mark 10:2–11; and Luke 16:18 that people should not divorce for just any trivial reason. In these passages, Christ plainly states that the only reason a man should divorce his wife is if she is sexually unfaithful to him—and vice versa. Mark 10:12 also says, "And if a woman divorces her husband and marries another, she commits adultery."

Jesus elaborates a bit more in Matthew 19:9, stating that fornication can be a grounds for divorce and when it is, remarriage by the innocent person is permitted and can be justified. Sexual unfaithfulness does give the innocent person the right to divorce the guilty person and marry a single or widowed person, or a person with a scriptural divorce.

Sexual unfaithfulness is not automatic grounds for divorce, but such action does make divorce an option. One act of unfaithfulness that is confessed and repented of does not always imply a totally immoral lifestyle, nor should it mean a hasty trip to the divorce court. That isn't said to soften the devastating affects an affair or even one incident of fornication may bring about, but God does forgive and these obstacles can sometimes be overcome. We should always look for ways to restore the marriage rather than for an excuse to end it.

A final thought on marital unfaithfulness is that you as a young Christian woman have the responsibility to choose a committed Christian as your husband, not someone else's unfaithful husband. While it is sometimes easy to fall for a married man, step back and think about it. No matter how it feels or what he tells you, the bottom line is that he's cheating on his wife. Even if he did marry you, what have you gained? Some other woman's unfaithful husband! If he was untrue to her, he will most likely be untrue to you. Don't accept this type behavior. You deserve the best!

What about Abusive Relationships?

Physical violence and abuse in a marriage is the ultimate example of un-Christlike behavior. While many problems can be overcome in a marriage, including unfaithfulness, abuse appears to fall into a different category. Men are commanded in Ephesians 5:25 to treat their wives with respect and to love them as Christ loved the church. In 1 Peter 3:7, husbands are also commanded to live with their wives in an understanding manner, as with a weaker vessel, since she is a woman. Although the husband is given the responsibility of being the head of the family, nothing or no one gives him the authority or right to physically abuse his wife.

A woman must use good judgment to defend and protect herself and the children if her husband becomes abusive and violent toward them. It is important that she connect with Christians or other friends to supply support if she finds herself in a dangerous situation or an abusive marriage. Would God expect a woman to sit by idly while she is abused or her children are beaten or killed?

In 1 Corinthians 7:11–15, Paul gives instructions to Christians about staying married to their unbelieving spouses. He encourages the Christian to stay with the unbelieving spouse so as to possibly convert him or her to Christ by their godly life and example. He does, however, give authority for the Christian spouse to leave the unbeliever if things become intolerable.

In verse 11 of this passage, Paul says that if the situation becomes intolerable and the wife decides to leave her husband, so be it, but she must remain unmarried or else be reconciled to her husband at a later time. Some misuse this passage of scripture to defend any situation they want to escape. However, from studying these verses it certainly appears reasonable that abusive relationships could fall into that intolerable category of which Paul speaks.

What to Do If Faced with a Divorce

Hopefully, divorce will never be a part of your life. Yet, in spite of everything, if you do find yourself facing a divorce, remember that Jesus always concentrated on the marriage rather than the divorce. Consider these suggestions if you're ever faced with divorce:

- *Don't Be So Quick to Throw in the Towel!* If another person is threatening the marriage, stop all communication and association with that person immediately. Take some time to think about the devastating consequences of divorcing, and don't be too hasty in making a decision that will affect the rest of your life.

- *Stay Focused on the Marriage and Its Good Times.* Don't dwell on the negatives. Remember the good times you shared with your husband, and remember his good qualities.

- *Take Some Time Alone.* Pray to God for understanding, wisdom, and guidance in making your decision.

- *Take Some Time Together.* If possible, spend some time alone with your husband and rekindle the interests that attracted you to him in the beginning.

- *Remember the Children.* Divorce will affect the children. Make sure the commitment to your family is a priority.

- *Seek Good Christian Counseling.* Both parties should be willing to discuss their problems and willing to try to resolve the issues.

- *Remember What the Bible Teaches about Remarriage.* If you are divorcing for reasons other than fornication, are you willing to remain unmarried for the rest of your life? Make sure you understand the seriousness and permanence of a decision to divorce when sexual unfaithfulness is not the cause for the divorce.

Conclusion

God's teachings concerning marriage, divorce, and remarriage can seem somewhat harsh and unfair, especially in today's society when so many people believe they are free to do whatever they feel is right. Sometimes we may not understand all we are commanded and instructed to do by the Bible, but we must trust in God that all will work out according to His will and purpose. A mature Christian woman will put her faith and assurance in the Lord and abide by His commandments.

Above all, we as Christian women should remember the forgiveness and love God offers when we fall short of our goals and aspirations in life, whether it is through divorce or some other failure in our lives. We should also remember God does have guidelines and commandments concerning divorce and remarriage, and we must respect those commandments and live by them, regardless of our opinions or personal situations.

No one should ever be proud of a divorce in any way or treat it in a flippant manner. God stands willing to forgive anyone who fails in marriage, and Christian divorcees should continue to serve God to the best of their ability. God loves everyone, whether divorced, single, or married, and there is a place for all in His church. As Christians, we should always strive to be compassionate and loving to those who are divorced. It's the Christ-like thing to do.

1. Under what circumstances is it permissible for a couple to separate? In case of separation, what are their alternatives?

2. Do you think a couple should stay together just for the sake of the children? Name some ways their staying together would be beneficial and some ways it would not be beneficial.

3. How does divorce affect children?

4. What should a woman do if she is in a marriage that is abusive? If she chooses to leave her husband, what are her options?

5. What does the Bible teach about divorce? How does God feel about it?

6. What causes affairs? If a married partner has an affair, is that an automatic grounds for divorce?

7. Name some plain, common-sense reasons not to date a married man or an unscripturally divorced man.

8. How should a divorced Christian woman conduct herself?

9. What are the biblical justifications for remarrying?

10. What do you believe to be the three primary causes of divorce?

CHAPTER NINE

Mother—To Be or Not To Be?

Compromising Motherhood

Fence-Straddling Position: "She's just a stay-at-home mom. She doesn't have a real job."

Bible Position: "The aged women likewise, that they be in behaviour as becometh holiness, not false accusers, not given to much wine, teachers of good things; that they may teach the young women to be sober, to love their husbands, to love their children, to be discreet, chaste, keepers at home, good, obedient to their own husbands, that the word of God be not blasphemed" (Titus 2:3–5 KJV).

Scripture Search

Exodus 20:12	Luke 1:42
Proverbs 31:10–31	Luke 2:48
Matthew 15:4	Luke 18:20
Matthew 19:19	1 Timothy 5:14
Mark 10:19	Titus 2:3–5

Say What?

Submission—To yield oneself to the authority or will of another. Humble and compliant.

Yield—Submit; defer; to surrender to another.

Virtuous—Morally excellent.

Moral—Conforming to a standard of what is right and good.

Chaste—Pure in thought and acts; modest. Refraining from acts, thoughts, or desires that are not virginal or sanctioned by marriage.

Discreet—Showing good judgment in conduct and especially in speech.

Sober—Marked by restraint, moderation, or seriousness; unhurried, calm.

"Latch-key Child"—A young child of working parents who must spend part of the day at home unsupervised.

Unconditional Love—Love given to another without limits, conditions, or restrictions, such as the love of a parent for a child or the love of God for all mankind.

Sacrifice—Something of value given up or lost, such as the blessing parents generously bestow upon their children.

It had been one of those days. As Jamie screeched to a halt at the traffic light, her heart was pounding and her patience was wearing a bit thin. It was already past three, and she knew eight-year-old twins, Dustin and Katie, would be wondering what had happened to her as they waited for her to pick them up at school. Kyle was strapped in the carrier in the back seat, asleep for now, but subject to waking hungry at any minute.

She had intended to get the car checked out, since it was making a funny sound when she braked. The oil needed changing, too. Her husband Jon had mentioned last week that his parents would be coming over for dinner tonight, so she had left a roast cooking in the oven at home.

How can I possibly get everything done and look half-way decent tonight? What am I going to wear? I hope the roast is good. I need to dust and vacuum when I get home. I need to take the clothes out of the dryer, too. I hope the kids behave. I think the kids' clothes are clean. There should be just enough time for a quick shower if I can get Katie to watch Kyle for a few minutes.

Why I am so tired? Jamie *suddenly wondered. It seemed impossible all these thoughts could be racing through her head while she sat through just one traffic light.*

As the light changed to green, she saw the billboard out of the corner of her eye and did a double-take to make sure she had read it right. It screamed at her: What Idiot Coined the Phrase "Stay-at-Home" Mom?

She laughed out loud as she accelerated and once again drove off—taxi driver, gourmet cook, cleaning lady, Super Mom.

It has been said that the hardest job a woman will ever do comes with no salary, no training, and no time off. It is often a lonely and thankless job, but the rewards and benefits are tremendous. It is the job of a being a mother.

The term *stay-at-home mom* is surely something of a misnomer. Since the mother doesn't have a job with a salary, the term implies she doesn't really work. How absurd! Every mother is a working woman, 24 hours a day.

In today's world, the concept of stay-at-home mothers is somewhat of an oddity and considered old-fashioned by many. Of course, it didn't used to be that way. Certainly times have changed since the '50s when it was typical for mothers to stay at home, but have we really gained much over the past 50 years? From 1940 to 1990, the percentage of kids with moms staying at home declined from 43 percent to only 18 percent.

One of the most emotional and controversial issues of our day is whether or not it is acceptable for a woman to work outside the home once she becomes a mother. The Bible doesn't prohibit women or mothers from working outside the home. There are several examples given of mothers and women working outside the traditional home scenario: the Virtuous Woman, Proverbs 31; Dorcas, Acts 9:36–42; Lydia, Acts 16:13–15; and others.

The Bible does teach that a woman should have her priorities in order and that she is to love her husband and children, be a keeper of the home, and subject to her husband (Proverbs 31; Titus 2:3-5). Are those notions too old fashioned for us in the twenty-first century? If so, why? Today, it seems we often belittle those women who make the decision to stay at home. There is an unfortunate, powerful social stigma concerning stay-at-home mothers, often relegating them to second-class citizens. Some people think a little less of these women because they don't have "a real job."

Some have even called the role of mother boring, unfulfilling, and stifling. In her book, *The Role of Women,* Betty Choate gives a different view:

> God could not have paid a higher or greater tribute to woman than giving her the privilege of shaping the lives and souls of the next generation and for eternity.

It is an incredible honor and privilege to be a mother. Christians should praise these women and support their decision to stay at home. Younger women should understand and appreciate the words written by Paul in Titus 2 that state being keepers at home is pleasing to God. Motherhood is a noble and important career and a position that should be elevated to a higher status.

What's Important to You?

For single young women or those married women without children, the greatest lesson to be derived from this study is understanding that one day you will likely have to make a decision about whether or not to have children. If you do have children, will you also have a career and work outside the home or will you stay at home? What do you want? What is important to you and your husband? What does God want you to do?

You can't stay neutral. You must get the facts to make a good decision, discuss it with your spouse or spouse-to-be, pray about it, and go for it! Avoid getting into the predicament many women find themselves today, struggling just to keep their heads above water. They can't do justice to either job whether they're at home or at the office, since they're stressed out to the point that each task becomes a monumental obstacle. Everyone suffers because of it.

What Does the Bible Say about Mothers?

There is something special about the word *mother*. For most of us, it evokes memories of happiness, joy, acceptance, and unconditional love. It seems as though the bond between a mother and child grows stronger, too, as the years go by.

Adding the word *Christian* to the word *mother* makes it even more special. I have been fortunate and blessed to have a Christian mother and fine, godly grandmothers to guide me in my life. I am reminded of the story of Timothy in 2 Timothy 1:5 and the Christian influence his mother, Eunice, and his grandmother, Lois, had on him as a young child. Mine definitely influenced me in the same manner.

The Bible is clear in its many examples that mothers are special and that motherhood is a privilege. Some of those examples are examined below:

- *Motherhood Is Honorable.* We are told in Matthew 19:19; Mark 10:19; and Luke 18:20 that motherhood is honorable and that we should honor our mothers. To honor means to hold one in highest esteem and respect. It denotes a feeling of reverence and a combination of liking, loving, and respecting a person. No word could better describe how we should feel toward our mothers.

- *Mothers Are Worthy of Praise.* To praise someone means to highly approve of and admire them. Proverbs 31:28 says of the virtuous woman: "Her children rise up and call her blessed; her husband also, and he praises her."

- *Mothers Are Women Who Are Blessed with Children.* Psalms 127:3 simply says that "children are a heritage from the Lord, the fruit of the womb is a reward." What an awesome gift to receive from the Lord!

- *Mothers Are Teachers.* Paul gives instructions to the older women in Titus 2:3–5 to teach the younger women to love their husbands and children, to be discreet and chaste, to be kind, to yield to their husbands—and to be good workers at home. Moms are the world's best teachers—in action and in word. Proverbs 1:8 admonishes us not to forget our mother's teachings.

- *Mothers Are Keepers at Home.* Keeper—what a small, easily understandable word. Or is it? Take a closer look. What is God really asking of women in Titus 2 when He says that we are to be keepers at home? The word *keeper* implies a protector of a fortress or castle— one who is watchful, strong, and secure. A keeper is a manager of a household and will make appropriate provisions for her family. The word also means being faithful to a cause, to watch over, defend and keep from harm, to maintain in an orderly condition, to be a supporter, and to be a homemaker. What an awesome responsibility and privilege God has bestowed on women!

A Typical Day?

Some believe that a housewife has nothing to do but keep the children and keep the house for the husband, so she has an endless amount of leisure time. She happily whips up gourmet dinners and takes a lot of naps. In her endless hours of freedom, she watches TV, reads, and organizes details for her family. Wrong! In reality, stay-at-home moms are incredibly busy, challenged, and resourceful women. Out of necessity, they become ingenious managers of finances, school activities, church functions, and monotenous daily—sometimes hourly—chores.

Days of reading stories to the children, taking them to the library, operating a "taxi service," watching ballgames, and going to music lessons become typical for a stay-at-home mom. She will answer hundreds of questions, change countless diapers, keep the house, cook the meals, and tend to sick kids.

Can such mundane things really fulfill a woman today? The tide seems to be turning somewhat, and many are now emphatically saying yes! A recent survey by Youth Intelligence, a New York trend-tracking and marketing firm, found that 68 percent of 3000 women surveyed between the ages of 18 and 34, said they would prefer domestic life to corporate life if they could afford it.

Reasons for Staying at Home

Why are some women today leaving prosperous and rewarding careers in order to be at home? Many reasons are given as to why they go home, but three always stand out. Most women say they need more time to do a proper job in managing the affairs of the household and to care for their husbands and children. The second reason they give is to spend more time with their children; in other words, to be there when they are growing up. And the third reason is to avoid the hassle and stress of trying to do too much and ending up not doing a good job either at the job or at home.

Advantages of Staying at Home

The advantages of staying home with the children are numerous. A full-time mother will raise her own child and enjoy the intangibles of seeing her baby's first smile, hearing the first word, and seeing the first step. She will have some control over her own time and can decide her own priorities.

A stay-at-home mom will have the opportunity to seek part-time employment from the home if that is best for her family. She will also have the opportunity to educate her children in the home if she and her husband decide that is appropriate for them.

- *Home Schooling*

  As recently as the early '80s, home schooling was considered somewhat radical, with only about 50,000 children then being educated outside of school. Home schooling is now legal and regulated in all 50 states and the District of Columbia. Today, it is conservatively estimated that 1.5 to 2 million children are being schooled at home. The rise in home schooling is being called one of the most significant social trends of the past half century.

  Parents choose home schooling for many reasons, including the perception of poor academic quality in traditional schools, concerns about violence, issues related to peer pressure, and religious and cultural beliefs. Research shows that home-schooled kids are not "emotionally deprived" from lack of interaction with others as some critics have argued, but rather are flourishing in their social and personal lives, in addition to achieving high academic marks.

  It's not an easy job to be a teacher-mom, but once again the rewards are many: thriving children who can develop their academic, athletic, and musical skills at their own pace in a friendly, non-threatening home environment; flexible schedules; and an unexpected family richness. Parents who choose to home school must expect to work hard in developing a curriculum for their children—developing musical, athletic, or other talents demonstrated in their children—while maintaining a stable and balanced network of friendships, as well as social and religious activities.

What a challenge for any parent to take upon themselves to home school! As a young woman, you have the opportunity now to take advantage of broadening your education and developing your skills to the maximum to prepare yourself for home schooling your children in the future if that is deemed best for your family.

• *Lifetime Rewards*

A stay-at-home mom will always have the satisfaction of knowing she invested as top priority the well-being of her children. As a mother and teacher, she will be totally involved in the most important position she will ever have—teaching her children to grow into adult Christians.

After all is said and done, it appears that the biggest practical advantage of being a full-time mother is that most women truly seem to enjoy this role that God has given them; it is the job she is cut out best to perform.

Disadvantages of Staying at Home

It would be unrealistic to assume everything will be rosy if a woman does choose to be a stay-at-home mom. The most obvious drawback of being a stay-at-home mom is that there's no paycheck. Since there is no paycheck, a full-time mom may of necessity become a master of juggling finances and careful budgeting so her family can live on one check. Her self-image may also suffer from not bringing in any money, and sometimes stay-at-home moms fear that they will lose their marketable skills should they decide to go back to work after the children are grown.

Another disadvantage is that she may have to overcome the social stigma in today's society of not having "a real job." If she is at home all day, she may lose touch with the outside world and become bored and lonely. It is important if a woman does stay home that she tries her best to develop friendships with other moms, since it would be unrealistic to expect her husband to fill all her social needs all the time.

Having It All—Except Children

Obviously, deciding whether or not to have children is a personal choice for each married couple. There are women who will never become mothers—some, because of their inability to bear children and others, because they choose not to.

Karen Peterson, in an April 2002 *USA Today* article, wrote of a group of women she calls "working non-mothers." She defines these women as those who have birthed successful careers, accumulated status, achieved comfortable incomes, but as those who never got around to having the one thing they always intended: a child. Many high-ranking executive women have awakened to the stark reality that in their quest and drive to make it to the top professionally, they essentially forgot to have a baby!

Sylvia Ann Hewlett, author of *Creating a Life: Professional Women and the Quest for Children,* based her book on a nationally representative survey of 1186 high-achieving women ages 28 to 55. Hewlett defines *high-achieving* as women whose incomes place them in the top 10 percent for their age group. The high achievers, ages 28 to 40, earned at least 55,000 dollars annually; those ages 41 to 55, earned at least 65,000 dollars a year.

Her findings were sobering and will hopefully be put to good use by young women who put off having a child—sometimes until it is too late:

- 33 percent of high-achieving women in general are childless at 40.
- 42 percent of women in corporate American are childless.
- 49 percent of "ultra achievers" (earning more then 100,000 dollars a year) are childless.
- 25 percent of childless high achievers ages 41 to 55 still would like a child.
- No high achievers ages 41 to 55 had a first child after age 39.
- Overall, only 11 to 14 percent of those without children preferred it that way.

Children truly add excitement and much happiness to a home. I am fortunate to have two sisters who have four children each—so I have the privilege of loving and associating with my five nephews and three nieces regularly. What a blessing!

As a single woman with no children, I am free to come and go as I please, but my decision not to have a child is one that I regret, and one that many women eventually regret as seen through results of various surveys. Childlessness is often unexpected and the majority of childless women say they always intended to have children. It is with that thought in mind that I offer the following story, written by an unknown author. Here, in part, is an article entitled "On Being a Mother."

We are sitting at lunch one day when my daughter casually mentions that she and her husband are thinking of starting a family. "We're taking a survey," she says half joking. "Do you think I should have a baby?"

"It will change your life," I say carefully, keeping my tone neutral.

"I know," she says. "No more sleeping in on weekends, no more spontaneous vacations . . ."

But that is not what I meant to tell her at all. I look at my daughter, trying to decide what to tell her. I want her to know what she will never learn in childbirth classes. I want to tell her that the physical wounds of childbearing will heal, but that becoming a mother will leave her with an emotional wound so raw that she will forever be vulnerable.

I consider warning her that she will never again read a newspaper without asking, "What if that had been my child?" That every plane crash, every house fire will haunt her. That when she sees pictures of starving children, she will wonder if anything could be worse than watching your own child die.

I look at her carefully manicured nails and stylish suit and think that no matter how sophisticated she is, becoming a mother will reduce her to the primitive level of a bear protecting her cub.

I feel I should warn her that no matter how many years she has invested in her career, she will be professionally derailed by motherhood. She might arrange for childcare, but one day as she is going into an important business meeting, she will think of her baby's sweet smell. She will have to use every ounce of her discipline to keep from running home, just to make sure her baby is all right. However decisive she may be at the office, she will second-guess herself constantly as a mother.

Looking at my attractive daughter, I want to assure her that eventually she will shed the pounds of pregnancy, but she will never feel the same about herself again. That her life, now so important, will be of less value to her once she has a child. I want her to know her relationship with her husband will change, but not in the way she thinks. I wish she could understand how much more you can love a man who is careful to powder the baby or who never hesitates to play with his child.

I want to describe to my daughter the exhilaration of seeing your child learn to ride a bike. I want to capture for her the belly laugh of a baby who is touching the soft fur of a dog or a cat for the first time. I want her to taste the joy that is so real, it actually hurts.

My daughter's quizzical look makes me realize that tears have formed in my eyes. "You'll never regret it," I finally say.

Then I reach across the table, squeeze my daughter's hand and offer a silent prayer for her, and for me, and for all of the mere mortal women who stumble their way into this most wonderful of callings—this blessed gift from God—that of being a mother.

Give Careful Thought

The decision to have children and work outside the home or to be a stay-at-home mother is one that each couple pray about and seek guidance from God in making the best choice. All the costs associated with working should be considered before embarking on a career, especially if young children are involved. Childcare costs, transportation expenses, clothing, food, and many other expenses can quickly eat up a paycheck.

Keep in mind, too, that a mom can't go back and relive those early days with her child after he or she has grown up. Now is the time for you as a young person to decide how you feel about this issue, listen to what God says in His word, and then do everything possible to make sure your dreams come true.

No woman should ever compromise her decision for being a stay-at-home mother or apologize for being just a mom. Motherhood is undoubtedly the most rewarding experience and role a woman can have. Mothers should be praised, honored, and revered for their work.

Consider this marvelous tribute to all mothers everywhere.

This tribute is for the mothers who didn't win Mother of the Year—for all the runners-up and all the wannabes: the mothers too tired to enter or too busy to care. This is for all the mothers who froze their buns off on metal bleachers at soccer games Friday night instead of watching from the cars, so that when their kids asked, "Did you see my goal?" they could say, "Of course, I wouldn't have missed it for the world" and mean it.

This is for all the mothers who have sat up with sick toddlers in their arms, wiping up barf laced with Oscar Mayer wieners and cherry Kool-Aid saying, "It's okay, honey, Mommy's here." This is for all the mothers of Kosovo who fled in the night and can't find their children. This is for the mothers who gave birth to babies they'll never see and for the mothers who took those babies and made them homes.

This is for all the mothers who run car pools and make cookies and sew Halloween costumes—and for all the mothers who don't. What makes a good mother anyway? Is it patience? Compassion? Broad hips? The ability to nurse a baby, fry a chicken, and sew a button on a shirt, all at the same time?

Or is it heart? Is it the ache you feel when you watch your son disappear down the street, walking to school alone for the very first time? The jolt that wakes you from sleep to dread, from bed to crib at 2:00 A.M. to put your hand on the back of a sleeping baby? The need to flee from wherever you are and hug your child when you hear news of a school shooting, a fire, a car accident, a baby dying? I think so.

So this is for all the mothers who sat down with their children and explained all about making babies—and for all the mothers who wanted to but just couldn't. This is for reading "Good Night, Moon" twice a night for a year. And then reading it again—"just one more time."

This is for all the mothers who mess up—who yell at their kids in the grocery store and swat them in despair and stomp their feet like a tired two-year-old who wants ice cream before dinner.

This is for all the mothers who taught their daughters to tie their shoe-laces before they started school—and for all the mothers who opted for Velcro instead. For all the mothers who bite their lips—sometimes until they bleed—when their 14-year-olds dye their hair green.

This is for all the mothers who show up at work with spit-up in their hair and milk stains on their blouses and diapers in their purses. This is for all the mothers who teach their sons to cook and their daughters to sink a jump shot.

This is for all mothers whose heads turn automatically when a little voice calls "Mom?" in a crowd, even though they know their own offspring are at home. This is for mothers who put pinwheels and teddy bears on their children's graves. This is for mothers whose children have gone astray, who can't find the words to reach them.

This is for young mothers stumbling through diaper changes and sleep deprivation—and mature mothers learning to let go. For working mothers and stay-at-home mothers; single mothers and married mothers.

This is for mothers, who despite all they have to deal with mentally and physically because of their own illnesses, give all they are capable of giving to their children for no other reason than love. For those mothers who deserve more credit than they ever will receive for all that they have given and accomplished.

This is for all those mothers who need to remember that no matter how their children choose to live their lives that they have done the best job they could, raised them to be the best adults they knew how to be, and thereby accomplished more than anyone could rightfully ever expected of them—because all anyone on this earth can do is their best.

This is for you all. So hang in there.

—Author Unknown

It's Your Turn!

1. Discuss a typical mother's motive for working outside the home. Does selfishness enter into that decision?

2. What are some ways a full-time mother can stay up to date on current trends and job skills?

3. How can a stay-at-home mom avoid boredom and depression from not being out in the real world?

4. Is it wrong for a woman to choose not to have children? Explain your answer.

5. How important is it for a mother to stay at home with her children?

6. Give examples of how you or a friend has been helped by a mother who stayed at home.

7. What does the Bible say about motherhood? What is unconditional love?

8. Do you think the Bible teaches that women must stay at home? Defend your answer.

9. Why are many women giving up successful careers to stay at home?

10. Why do you think society has pictured stay-at-home mothers as second-class citizens? What are some ways to correct that?

CHAPTER TEN

You Go, Girl!

Compromising Our Talents

Fence-Straddling Position: "I just don't think I can learn to do that. I'm not very talented. God didn't bless me with any talents. It's not that important anyway."

Bible Position: "As each one has received a gift, minister it to one another, as good stewards of the manifold grace of God" (1 Peter 4:10).

Scripture Search

Exodus 35:25–26   Matthew 25:14–28
Proverbs 31:10–31   Acts 9:36
Ecclesiastes 9:10   Romans 12:6
1 Peter 4:10

Say What?

Talent—A capacity for achievement or success. A natural ability or aptitude that requires development.

Gift—A special ability for doing something, usually implying a special favor by God.

Ability—Talent, special skills, or competence in an activity or occupation.

Leadership—Ability to lead, guide, or direct another.

Aptitude—Readiness in learning; intelligence. Capability. A natural liking for some activity and the likelihood for success in it.

Confident—Sure of oneself. Having strong beliefs and full assurance of something.

Perseverance—Continue on steadfastly. To maintain a purpose in spite of difficulties or obstacles.

Aggressive—Forceful, pushy. A disposition to dominate or to master.

Assertive—Bold and confident—usually in a manner that is not considered offensive or too aggressive.

Ambition—An earnest desire for some type of achievement or distinction.

Opportunity—A good chance for self-advancement. A favorable condition for attaining a goal.

"Kelly," Mrs. Henderson said. "Our congregation's ladies' workshop is coming up in May, and the committee wants you to be our speaker!"

No way! Kelly panicked, then quickly regained her composure. "Oh, I'd be happy to help with the convention, Mrs. Henderson, but there is no way I can be your speaker!"

Mrs. Henderson was undaunted. "So many of our ladies have known you over the years, and we feel you are the right person for the job. We are expecting a lot of the younger women to attend the convention, and I know you will connect with them perfectly. Our theme this year is Friendship. *I'm sure you'll do just fine."*

Kelly's thoughts raced. What am I going to say now? I can never do this, I'm too young, I can't talk before groups, I will look foolish, I'm too nervous, I don't have anything to say.

Wait! *Kelly interrupted herself.* This is exactly what happened at work last month! *Kelly recalled how she had argued with her supervisor over an important briefing he wanted her to present to the entire office staff. Kelly had point-blank refused to do it, but she lost the argument after her supervisor told her in no uncertain terms she would give that briefing.*

The funny thing was that Kelly didn't faint as she thought she would, and she didn't die as she said she would. She had pushed herself to give the briefing, she had prepared herself by studying her material, and she had won high praise for her efforts. Could she do it again?

"Mrs. Henderson," Kelly began. "I feel inadequate, but I am pleased by the invitation. Let me think about this for a few days. Maybe I can do this after all."

As Kelly walked away, she thought, With the help of God and a little practice and study, surely this might be possible after all!

What's Your Talent?

So what does this story have to do with talents? For one thing, Kelly's successful briefing presentation convinced her that she could do things she didn't think she could. For another, it taught her the importance of pushing herself to grow.

Developing our talents will require getting out of our comfort zones and taking some risks. Kelly's natural talent wasn't public speaking, so she shied away from it whenever possible. The point is she learned to speak before groups, even though she might never be totally comfortable doing so.

Everyone has talents, regardless of how insignificant they may seem. Some young women hide their talents, and some women are afraid to use their talents, fearing failure and possibly rejection. Others are lazy, and some don't know what their talents are.

On the other hand, many young women are emerging today with great confidence, eager to take on any challenge, and ready to use their talents to the best of their abilities.

For a successful and happy life, we must branch out, take risks, learn what our talents are, and develop them. We must not compromise our God-given talents or abilities; we must be receptive to new experiences and ideas. Change is inevitable and usually good, but changing our behavior and thought patterns is not always easy.

Opportunities Galore

For young women today who choose to use their talents to become a wife and mother or to enter the workforce, the sky is the limit. Either choice, it is a wonderful time to be a woman! Since the '70s, dramatic changes have occurred for women. The Equal Employment Opportunity (EEO) laws enacted during that era helped advance women's pay and job opportunities. And opportunities abound for the woman who makes home and family her career.

A young woman who chooses a professional career can now more easily become a doctor instead of the nurse she would have been encouraged to become a generation ago. She can be a manager or a supervisor. The door is wide open for female athletes to become professionals. Great strides have also been made for women in salary potential and pay equality.

A young woman who chooses to become a wife and mother also has advantages and opportunities that perhaps were not available to her mother or grandmother. She can use her talents in decorating, managing, and keeping a warm and inviting home. She has the opportunity to be a teacher to her children in every sense of the word. The computer has opened doors for her to use her talents in starting up and managing a part-time business or communicating with others through email.

What does all this have to do with you as a young Christian woman? Simply this: keep your options open as you grow up! Is it your desire to be a mother and stay at home with your children, bringing them up in the Lord? Do you want to go to college? Is obtaining a professional degree or title a high priority for you? Do you want a career or merely a job to bring in some extra cash for a short time? What skills do you need to develop to support yourself if you remain single or were to become single after a divorce or death of your husband? Do you want to work in missions? Do you see the need in the church for an outstanding Bible teacher?

Other questions are also important. If you choose to work outside the home, are you working out of true necessity or because you want a bigger loaf of bread? The final and most important question is this: What does God want you to do? Can you best serve Him in the workplace or by establishing a home and focusing on your family? Pursuing God's will can save you a lot of heartache over the years.

The Bible teaches in Ecclesiastes 9:10 that regardless of our decision, whatever our hands find to do, we should do our best. We should all try to develop and use our talents, whatever they are, to the best of our ability.

The Career Woman

Opportunities for exciting careers and lucrative salaries are available today for those women who are willing to work for them. Women can now take advantage of these exceptional opportunities that were not available to them just 20 or 30 years ago. However, it is easy to fall into the trap of single-mindedly pursuing a career, climbing the ladder, and losing sight of priorities. Satan lurks, encouraging Christian women to chase career advancement to the neglect of spiritual growth and family matters.

A career is not always what is it advertised to be. It can become the same thing every day—a monotonous daily rut with little time off, never-ending deadlines, and extensive travel. Women discover they often have to work very long and hard to gain respect and financial rewards in the business world.

In choosing a career, it is also important to understand that money should not always be the deciding factor as to which field to enter. Service or teaching jobs should not be ignored just becasue they might not pay as much as other professions. It is important to find a job that is compatible with Christian living and one that will bring happiness and fulfillment, as well as pay the bills.

Opportunities also abound for Christian women to set a good example in our job situations, whatever they are. In Matthew 5:14, Christ said His disciples are to be the light of the world. We can do that by performing our jobs in a competent and professional manner, being assertive without being aggressive, and by always conducting ourselves in a Christ-like manner by not participating in the numerous worldly activities that are readily available in the workplace—gossiping, stealing, cheating, and sexual affairs.

Just because a woman is a stay-at-home wife and mother doesn't mean she is exempt from temptation either. A woman working at home is faced with the daily challenges of temper loss, telephone gossip, wasting time, engaging in affairs, and many of the same worldly activities as in the workplace. Any job has its pitfalls; a wise woman will anticipate these and emerge victorious.

A final and sobering thought: married career women have the second highest divorce rate of any other group, the first being those on welfare. Wise decisions should be made before taking on a full-time career, especially when children are involved.

Working Mothers

Sometimes mothers are criticized for working outside the home and for not staying at home with their children. Yet it seems as though society has almost dictated that many mothers seek outside employment just to make ends meet. The Bible does not prohibit mothers from working outside their home, but it does command a wife to be a keeper at home.

The virtuous and multi-talented woman in Proverbs 31 was one such working woman. Note, though, that she did have her priorities in order, since she first took care of her family; her work was never a hindrance. She was self-employed—buying, manufacturing, and selling goods. Her work revolved around her family—she was in a position to make it so.

Other women of example—and probably mothers—who are mentioned in the Bible are Deborah, who led Israel as a judge, prophetess, and military commander (Judges 4 and 5); Phoebe, a wealthy servant and helper in the apostle Paul's ministry (Romans 16:1); Dorcus, a Christian servant who made clothing and robes for others (Acts 9: 36–42); Lydia, an influential merchant and business woman from the city of Thyatira (Acts 16:14); Anna, a prophetess (Luke 2:36), and Priscilla, a tentmaker and a teacher of the gospel (Acts 18).

Christians should be careful about criticizing working mothers, since we have not walked in their shoes or may not know their exact circumstances. As with others, these women have their own special reasons for working. Financial necessity it often the biggest factor, and bringing home a paycheck is one of the biggest reasons given for working outside the home. Many others work to earn extra money for expenses such as funding a child's college education. Others cite personal fulfillment, contribution to society, recognition, and status as reasons for working.

Some women, such as single mothers or those abandoned or divorced, have no choice other than to work to provide for themselves and their children. Use your talents and abilities to give these women a break. Whenever possible, offer to cook a meal, baby-sit, or mow a lawn without charge.

Instead of being critical, we should look for ways to help a working mom spend more time with her children. With the world's pressure on women to have more material things, many mothers who have never been encouraged to have less of the world's goods—houses, cars, clothes—will appreciate your encouragement and assistance.

Pitfalls of Working Mothers

Many women experience tremendous guilt and suffer low self-esteem over leaving their children in childcare facilities or leaving them home as latch-key kids. Finding quality childcare that is affordable has become a major issue for families where the mother holds an outside job.

The stress and pressures of coping with both a career and family is difficult. I've listened to tale after tale from moms who have chosen to work outside the home. Time and again, their words echo the same message. Listen to one of them:

> It's like having two jobs, I'm always late, I'm always tired, I'm always behind. I don't seem to have time to do anything well, and I never seem to complete anything. I'm constantly worried, and I feel guilty when I leave my baby at the daycare center. Daycare is expensive, but I want to give my child the best care I can afford. Both my child and I are so tired at the end of the day. I'm just going through the motions, until I can get her to bed. There's no time to really talk. I have zero time for my husband and our conversations have dwindled to nearly nothing. I'm the mother, and I should be making my child feel safe, but I'm not. I'm on call 24 hours a day. My job is a mess too. I constantly worry that I will be called from the job to get my sick

child. I can no longer stay late at work to finish unexpected tasks and traveling has become a nightmare, trying to find someone to take care of my family while I'm away. Someone please help me—I just need some rest!

Is this an extreme case? No, these are real words from one mother who is trying her best to raise her children and work outside the home. This personal testimony reinforces that it's tough to be a mother, wife, and career woman. Can women indeed "have it all" as we've been lead to believe? Perhaps—but it will always come at a high cost. Are you willing to pay that price?

Suggestions for a Successful Career

In supervising both men and women over the past years, I've observed certain critical characteristics of those who have successful careers. These characteristics apply to homemakers as well. Consider the following:

- *Attitude.* A good employee, wife, or mother must be willing to do her best and take advantage of opportunities that are presented to her. A know-it-all and hard-to-get-along-with woman will never be an asset to her company or her family. Humility goes a long way, as does having a good sense of humor and self-confidence.

- *Aptitude.* This is simply the ability to learn how to do a job. Whether a woman's work is in her home or in an office, she must continually learn new skills.

- *Ability.* Successfully performing daily tasks requires that a person refine and polish basic characteristics such as effective communication, speaking before groups, computer proficiency, conscientious time management, and continuing education.

- *Appreciation.* A good associate is appreciative of her job, her opportunities, and her salary. A woman who chooses her family as a career and then whines and complains about her job will reap isolation. A griping, unappreciative employee does not display a Christ-like attitude.

Tips for a Successful Christian Career Woman

It is just as easy to blend in with an adult society as it is to adapt in school situations. In Romans 12:2, Paul tells us to not be conformed to this world, but to be transformed by the renewing of our minds. We should not be shaped into the world's mold, but rather have something special about us as Christians that the world will be able to see. Letting our lights shine at home or at work projects the image of Christ. Let's conduct ourselves in a professional and Christ-like manner.

- *Be an Example in Speech.* Cursing, talking loudly, losing our tempers, and telling crude jokes or stories are sure ways to draw negative attention to ourselves and set a bad example to all around us. Speaking kind and encouraging words to those we deal with daily is often as influential as any form of teaching for Christ.

- *Be Competent and Dependable.* Simply put, we should be a good example—showing up for work on time, leaving on time, and doing a day's work for a day's pay. When our home is our work, we are just as accountable for time management and honesty. We need to be students of our vocations, always striving for maximum efficiency.

- *Be Modest.* We should strive to be modest in our dress and about our accomplishments. Plunging necklines, bare midriffs, short skirts, and tight pants will always attract attention. But is this a reflection of Christ inside me? And when I toot my own horn, others want to cover their ears. We should never be boastful, but rather let others praise us (Proverbs 27:2).

- *Be Willing to Help Others.* We should be willing to share our knowledge with those around us and never be too good to help others.

- *Work for the Lord.* Remember, whatever our jobs, we are essentially working for the Lord—so we should always do our best!

Developing Our Talents for Service in the Church

In addition to using our talents to the best of our ability in the secular workplace or in the home, we should also look for ways to use our talents to the glory of God to the best of our ability. In Romans 12, Paul told the Roman Christians:

Having then gifts differing according to the grace that is given to us, let us use them: if prophecy, let us prophesy in proportion to our faith; or ministry, let us use it in our ministering; he who teaches, in teaching; he who exhorts, in exhortation; he who gives, with liberality; he who leads, with diligence; he who shows mercy, with cheerfulness (Romans 12:6–8).

If God gave these miraculous gifts for His glory, doesn't it seem logical that He also gives us talents for His glory? However, too many Christians seem to believe God needs only teachers and leaders in the church, that He does not need other tasks performed. Teaching and being an effective leader are great characteristics, no doubt about it. But take a closer look. Paul also says those who have the gift of encouraging should encourage. Our talent may be that of encouraging others, either by a kind word or a card. That can be just as important as teaching!

Nothing would ever get done in the church if everyone had the same talents. We should be thankful for our talents, however insignificant we may see them, and use them for the glory of God. Keep in mind that there are many areas in which we can serve. We should not sell ourselves short—perhaps we can teach. Don't automatically reject the idea. Learning to develop our God-given talents will require time and effort, but the benefits are tremendous.

How to Develop Talents

The following suggestions for developing your talents may apply in the business world, in your home, in your service to the Lord, or in your personal life. Try them!

- *Identify What Really Excites and Motivates You.* If you enjoy a particular activity, you probably have a talent in that area. Maybe you like to sing, write, or teach and could develop those talents more fully. However, do not automatically discount those you may not be as comfortable doing.

- *Practice, Practice, Practice!* Take advantage of every opportunity you have to improve and refine your skills. Develop your talents to the best of your ability.

- *Take a Few Risks.* Be willing to be less than perfect. Developing your talents will mean taking a few chances. Learn from your failures.

- *Learn to Laugh at Yourself.* Expect some failures along the way while you are developing your talents; and remember, it isn't the end of the world to fail at times. Develop a thick skin, a good sense of humor, and don't take yourself so seriously.

- *Keep a Positive Attitude.* Remember that everyone is human, and people do not normally want you to fail. Friends and family can become your biggest supporters as you improve your abilities.

- *Take Advantage of the Opportunities Available to Women Today.* Many more opportunities are available to young women today than were available just a generation ago. Take advantage of these opportunities to be all that you can be. Study, continue your education, read, and never stop learning. Rewarding and important work waits for women in the church. Take the initiative to find out what needs to be done and do it.

- *Develop the Spirit and Attitude of a Servant.* Jesus was the ultimate example of the obedient and kind servant. Nothing was too small or menial for Him to do. Can you imagine the Son of God actually washing the dirty feet of his disciples? Yet, that's what He did. Christians should also have this same spirit and not be so concerned with who gets the credit for a job. Try never to act as though some task is too small or beneath you.

- *Get Out of Your Comfort Zone.* For years I hid my talents behind the mask of shyness, and I found it hard to break out of that shell. You, too, may have to work extremely hard to get out of your comfort zone and overcome certain shortcomings. Be willing to try, and you will be consistently surprised by the results.

- *Trust in the Lord.* If you are strong, attractive, and talented it may be easier to trust in yourself rather than trusting in God who gave you those gifts. Remember to thank God for what you are and what you have so your trust does not become misplaced.

- *Use It or Lose It.* The Bible teaches that the Lord will take away your talents if you don't use them. In the *Parable of the Talents* in Matthew 25, Jesus tells the story of a man who entrusted his property to his servants while he was away on a trip. To one man, he gave ten talents of money, to another two talents, and to the other man, only one talent. The ten-talent man and the two-talent man invested theirs wisely and doubled their money, but the one-talent man was afraid and hid his in the ground. When the master returned from his trip, he was displeased with the one-talent servant and called him wicked and lazy. He took back the talent he had given to that servant and gave it to the ten-talent man. The one-talent man was selfish and self-centered. Always be careful not to hide your talents, whatever they may be, or the Lord may take them away. It is not how many talents you have, but how you use them that is important.

It's Your Turn!

1. Discuss some ways you can develop your talents.

2. Are people born with certain talents or must they be developed?

3. What are some advantages and disadvantages for mothers working outside the home?

4. What are some important characteristics to assure a successful career?

5. Discuss Romans 12:6–8 and tell how it is important to the subject of talents.

6. Tell the class of your feelings as the child of a working mom or a full-time mom.

7. What are some obstacles a Christian woman may encounter by working outside the home?

8. How does society discourage a Christian teen from desiring a career as wife and mother?

9. What are some practical ways to help a working mother ease her workload?

10. Why are unused talents lost?

CHAPTER ELEVEN

Feminist Woman Versus Christian Woman

Compromising Our Feminine Roles

Fence Straddling Position: "I don't see anything wrong with women preaching or publicly serving in the church. We can do just as well or better than the men. Get with it—this is the twenty-first century!"

Bible Position: "Let a woman learn in silence with all submission. And I do not permit a woman to teach or to have authority over a man, but to be in silence. For Adam was formed first, then Eve. And Adam was not deceived, but the woman" (1 Timothy 2:11–14).

Scripture Search

Proverbs 31:10–31   Ephesians 5:21
Acts 16:14   1 Corinthians 14:33–35
Romans 12:6–8   1 Timothy 2:11–14
Galatians 3:26–28   1 Timothy 3:1-13
Titus 1:5-9

Say What?

Role—The proper and customary function of a person or thing.

Feminine—Female; woman. Having qualities of gentleness or delicacy.

Feminist—A woman or man who believes in and supports feminism—the theory of political, economic, and social equality of the sexes.

Submissive—Unresistingly and humbly obedient; yielding.

Virtuous—Morally excellent. Upright, chaste.

Domineering—Overbearing, forceful, controlling, bossy.

Usurp—To seize and hold a position, office, or power by force or without legal right.

Independent—Self-reliant; not relying on others for aid or support. Not influenced or controlled by others in matters of opinion or conduct.

Patriarchal—The male head of a family or tribal line. Father.

Authority—The right and power to command, decide, rule, or judge.

"Hi, Laura," Karen greeted her old friend as she finished her shopping. "It's been a while now, hasn't it?"

"You've got that right," smiled Laura.

Laura and Karen had grown up together and attended the same church for many years. Laura had always held a special place in Karen's heart as a kind-hearted Christian lady.

"Are you still worshiping at the Midway congregation?" Karen inquired.

"Well, no, actually my family has started attending another congregation over on the other end of town. We love it, too." Laura went on to explain. "The church there just seems to be more pro-gressive and modern than Midway—if you know what I mean."

"How so?" asked Karen, curiously.

"Oh, things are just different," Laura explained. "For one thing, there's more work for us women to do—you know—something more than just preparing food. I'm sorry, but I got so tired of that all the time.

Karen laughed at her old friend's newly found spirit. "Well, I guess we all feel that way sometimes. So what kind of work are you doing since you're not cooking anymore?"

Laura replied hesitantly, "I know it will be hard for you to believe, but I'm talking about 'real' work within the church—you know, leading singing, leading prayers, and teaching adult classes comprised of both men and women."

"You mean the women are publicly leading in the worship there?" asked Karen.

"That's right!" exclaimed Laura. "And get this—during the next year, we are expecting that some of the women will be asked to serve as deacons. Who knows, we may be asked to be elders one day, too. One step at a time!"

Laura continued, "I am really excited! Something about it just seems right, you know—the timing is right. I know it goes against all we were taught growing up in the church, but I just can't see anything wrong with this. We've got to catch up with the times— or I believe the church will die."

"Well, I don't know . . ." Karen struggled to find her tongue. "Maybe, you're right . . . I guess I might need to do a little more studying about it. It doesn't seem as though it's hurting anything . . . I can't imagine God would disapprove of anyone trying to serve Him. Maybe it doesn't really matter . . ."

Growing up during the height of "women's lib," I sympathized somewhat with the women's movement, though I did not call myself a feminist. Today as a single, professional career woman, I am grateful for some of the much-needed changes that the women's movement helped bring about, especially those changes in the workplace.

During the early '70s, radical feminist groups were also involved in trying to change society's views on women's roles in general. Their agenda looked good for young girls and women wishing to break out into the world then. As a young female athlete in those days, I was very much interested in such legislation as Title IX, the 1972 Education Amendment that opened the door for girls to participate in equally funded athletics in schools and colleges.

I wanted the opportunity to participate in sports and obtain athletic scholarships, just like the guys. I wanted to be equal with the men, I wanted an opportunity to be all I could be, and I wanted the good jobs. I wanted it all.

And I got it, along with a lot of other women. Sixty-five million women worked in careers in 1999 and comprised approximately 46 percent of the workforce. By 2008, it is expected that half of the workforce will be women. What have we gained? Perhaps plenty in terms of career choices, better paying jobs, and increased self-esteem. But the better question may be: At what cost have we gained this?

Many working women are mothers riddled with guilt over leaving their children in daycare facilities. They essentially work two or more jobs since they have their career, plus their work at home. Many business women have made their careers the top priority in life and have all but forgotten what's really important. Everywhere you look, women and mothers are frantically climbing the career ladders. Stress is up, patience is down, and women are constantly being pushed to excel—to do more. Has it been worth it? I wonder.

The Feminist Woman

The image radical feminists exhibit by pushing for power, dominating men and other women at any cost, and mocking God-ordained marriage roles does not exemplify the spirit of Christ. A Christian woman can certainly support equality of pay and fair and equal treatment in the workplace, but the principles and attitudes encouraged by many feminists do not portray the submissive, quiet demeanor God loves.

To illustrate, consider the following quotes from some of the world's leading radical feminists:

"For the sake of those who wish to live in equal partnership, we have to abolish and reform the institution of marriage."

Gloria Steinem, Co-founder and Editor
Ms. Magazine

"When they [conservative Christians] say men should take responsibility, they really mean men should take control . . . that men should be heads and masters of their families, and women should take a back seat. That is a very bad message as far as I am concerned."

Patricia Ireland, President
National Organization of Women (NOW)

"Radical elemental feminism is the politics and philosophy of the twentieth-first century . . . I encourage all 'wild women' participants to leave patriarchal institutions, which all churches are. We need the courage to sin. To sin is to be—to be ourselves."

Mary Daly
Author, scholar and one of the "mothers"
of the '60s and '70s feminist movement

The Virtuous Woman

Do any of those women sound like the virtuous woman mentioned in Proverbs 31? There an opposite picture is portrayed of the ideal woman. So much has been written about the woman in Proverbs that she has become a joke in some circles, since she appears to be a description of Super Woman instead of the virtuous woman.

But in the beautiful passage of Proverbs 31:10–31, she is aptly described as a hard worker, one who was not afraid of working with her hands. She was an intelligent woman worth more than rubies, who honored her husband by taking care of her family. She didn't waste her time, but was busy with her family and also her outside interests. This virtuous woman was smart, ambitious, industrious, and faithful to her husband and children. She had her priorities in order. What an example for women today!

Go for It?

Because of the societal changes brought about in part by the women's movement, young women today have more opportunities available to them than women did a few years ago, both in the business world and in their personal lives. In so many ways, young women today are ready to take on any challenge, to "go for it," and to succeed in whatever field they choose, whether a full-time mother or a professional career woman.

This wave of confidence and society's view that a woman can indeed do anything a man can do has undoubtedly brought confusion to Christian women in their perception of what they can do in service for the Lord and the church. On one hand, it seems as though we are always pushing and striving to develop our talents and being very good at what we do in the secular world, and then feel we have to put on our brakes when it comes to serving in the Lord's church. Is there an answer to this dilemma?

What Is Our Role in the Church?

Today's society tells us it is permissible for women to preach in public worship services, lead public prayer, and hold leadership positions in the church, such as that of an elder or deacon. After all, we have excelled as mothers, students, athletes, and business women. We've got our act together.

Some may ask, "Why can't women hold leadership positions in the church?" Are we being forced to compromise our talents by not being allowed to lead in worship or to hold leadership positions within the church? No! We must go to the Word of God to understand and accept our role of submission.

The whole issue of submitting to men has left many women with a bad taste in their mouths because some men have misunderstood the male role. Abuse of women is not uncommon; men sometimes misuse their authority. Though tragic and unfortunate, it is no reason not to have a submissive attitude toward God. Submission by both men and women is very scriptural. Ephesians 5:21 says, "Submitting to one another in the fear of God."

We must remember that God's restraint on female leadership in the church has nothing to do with intelligence, ability, or desire to serve God. It has everything to do with submission, obedience, and acceptance of God's overall plan for man, woman, marriage, and the church. The issues of submission and women's leadership roles hold great potential to divide the church in the near future, and compromising the truth that is taught in the Bible could drastically change the face of church leadership as we know it today.

What Does the Bible Teach?

Although women's role in public worship is controversial, biblical instruction is as relevant today as it was for the first-century church. The society in which we live may scoff at the seemingly old-fashioned teaching of male spiritual leadership in the church; yet, that is just what the Bible teaches. God's Word is the authority and final answer to our questions. Let's examine three scriptures normally cited when studying women's role in the church and determine how they apply today.

- *Galatians 3:28*

> There is neither Jew nor Greek, there is neither slave nor free, there is neither male nor female; for you are all one in Christ Jesus.

This verse is the most often misused scripture in the Bible in defense of women's equality. Most feminists quote this verse to justify women taking a lead in public worship service and in assuming leadership positions in the church. After all, this verse does say, "In Christ, there is no difference . . . between male and female . . . you are all the same in Christ Jesus."

However, this verse is taken out of context if trying to justify women's equality in church leadership positions. Paul is not talking about the role of women in the church at all. The entire book of Galatians deals with new Jewish Christians trying to force their old religious practices of Judaism on the new Gentile Christians. In other words, Paul was concerned about the continued requirement of certain Jewish customs and laws, such as circumcision for male believers in addition to baptism, not the role of women in the church.

Galatians 3:28 set forth an important new concept for the first-century believers and continues to be for us today. It simply means that each person, male or female, comes to God through a personal faith and not on the coattails of another person, such as a husband.

Women, in particular, would no longer have their identity with God based upon male-oriented lineage (patriarchy) and the exclusively male symbol of circumcision. The whole message Paul is giving is that one's race, position, or sex was no longer a barrier to identify with God. What an awesome message and how relevant it still is today! But it has nothing to do with women's public leadership in the church.

- *1 Corinthians 14:34–35*

  Let your women keep silent in the churches, for they are not permitted to speak; but they are to be submissive, as the law also says. And if they want to learn something, let them ask their own husbands at home; for it is shameful for women to speak in church.

The word *silent* used in this verse actually means "don't speak." Does this mean women should not talk at all during church services? If that is the case, then it would be wrong for a woman to sing during worship or make oral confession of her belief in Christ before the congregation, and we're commanded to do those things elsewhere in the Scriptures.

Keep in mind that the first-century church did not have the written Word as we do today, and the gifts of prophesying and speaking in tongues were given by God to both men and women during that time to get His message to the world. Imagine the confusion and noise when all these Christians met together and were prophesying and speaking in tongues simultaneously.

Paul was telling them that there were times when there should be silence, period!—by both men and women. Otherwise, what good was being done? Who could even understand what was being said? He further states in 1 Corinthians 14:33 that God is not the "author of confusion," and in verse 40 he says that all things in the church should be done "decently and in order."

None of this means Christian women in those days were inferior to men, nor does it mean that today. Certainly, women are just as spiritually insightful as men. Women are as educated and intelligent as men are. They make great leaders.

However, in the beginning God set things up with God as the head of Christ, Christ as the head of the church, and man as the head of woman (1 Corinthians 11:3; Ephesians 1:22).

In spiritual matters, God designated man as the spiritual leader and woman as submissive. This is how God designed it, and we must respect that. There is nothing degrading or belittling about the principle of submission; a quiet demeanor shows awe and respect. Once both men and women understand and accept our individual roles, our lives will be peaceful and orderly, and will be great blessings as we fulfill our God-given roles.

- *1 Timothy 2:11–14*

  Let a woman learn in silence with all submission. And I do not permit a woman to teach or to have authority over a man [usurp authority KJV], but to be in silence. For Adam was formed first, then Eve. And Adam was not deceived, but the woman . . ."

The word *usurp* means "to seize and hold a position, office, or power of office by force or without legal right." Paul says that women are not to assume leadership positions or have authority over men. Does this mean women can't teach? Of course not! However, women must not have authority when men are present. God delegated the role of church authority to men.

A question sometimes arises: If the elders or another man were to give a woman permission to teach over men or to be in a position of authority—that is, he doesn't care and wouldn't consider it usurping his authority—would it then be acceptable for the Christian woman to lead a public prayer, teach a mixed-gender Bible class, or become a deacon or an elder?

The answer must again be no. This simply goes against the basic biblical principle of male spiritual headship and God's plan from the beginning. Women are not to even possess the authority of spiritual leadership, regardless of how we may go about getting that permission. Only God can give permission of authority—not an elder and not another man—and God has not done this. All this doesn't mean women can't teach. It is just saying a woman can't teach or have authority over Christian men.

"Submission" and "Silence": Biblical or Cultural?

In studying these verses, it might be tempting to assume this instruction to women was cultural and applicable to those times and not relevant today. On the contrary, the culture in which Paul gave those commands was one that not only gave women the right to be seen and heard in public, but also recognized them as leaders in many aspects of religious life.

So, essentially, Paul was saying that in spite of, or regardless of, what culture said women could or could not do, it is forbidden by God for women to fill the role of public teacher in the assembly—simply because she's a woman. It is God's way and God's universal law from the beginning. It has nothing to do with culture or anything else such as a woman's ability, intelligence, or willingness, but it has everything to do with authority.

What Difference Does It Make?

Are these verses simply notions from the past? Aren't things different today? Does any of this matter to God anyway, as long as we worship and serve Him in our own way? Yes, it matters to Him! Many examples throughout the Bible show disastrous consequences when people assumed doing things their way did not make a difference.

In the opening chapters of the Bible, Cain found out the hard way how important obedience was. God instructed Cain and his brother Abel how to offer their sacrifices to Him and what was pleasing to Him. Abel offered his sacrifice as God had commanded; Cain did not. God accepted Abel's offering and rejected Cain's. What difference did it make? Cain still offered a good sacrifice. The problem was that he did it in his own way and not according to God's instructions, and God was displeased.

In 2 Samuel 6:1–17 we meet Uzzah, a man who was struck dead by God because of a seemingly minute infraction. At first glance, the story seems harsh. Poor Uzzah—all he did was reach out and try to keep the ark of the covenant from falling to the ground.

However, God had commanded that Levite priests put carrying poles through the corner rings of the ark and transport it without touching it. No one was to touch it, because it was holy. But there the children of Israel went, with King David as their leader, doing what *they* decided was best—carrying the ark on an oxcart. When the oxen stumbled, Uzzah reached out his hand to keep the ark from falling. What difference did that make? It made a lot of difference to God. He said not to touch it, and Uzzah did. God struck him dead.

God has given explicit instructions throughout the Bible of how he wants us to live our lives, how to become Christians, and how to worship and serve Him. He commands us to love our neighbors as ourselves. That means to do just that. He commands us to believe on Jesus as His son, repent of our sins, and be baptized in order to be saved. Does that mean we are free to choose what commandments we want to obey and ignore the others? No. It does make a difference what we believe and obey! We must be careful that we don't interject our own desires and preferences into obeying, worshiping, and serving God.

As a final thought, among the last verses in the Bible, Revelation 22:18–19 gives this sobering warning to those who would tamper with God's Word:

> For I testify to everyone who hears the words of the prophecy of this book: If anyone adds to these things, God will add to him the plagues that are written in this book; and if anyone takes away from the words of the book of this prophecy, God shall take away his part from the Book of Life, from the holy city, and from the things which are written in this book.

Where Do We Draw the Line?

Another issue to consider is if a woman could indeed do "something publicly," where do we draw the line? What is the acceptable limit for what we can do in public worship? Is it all right for us to make the announcements or to pass the communion trays? What about teaching a mixed-gender Bible class?

Would we draw the line when it came to our serving as elders or preachers? Would those roles be reserved just for the men, with the women performing less prominent roles? Wouldn't that way of thinking just make matters worse or more demeaning than some already perceive it to be?

God expects and wants all His followers to be submissive, but He especially wants women to be submissive to men when it comes to the home and spiritual leadership. It's the way He designed it. Submissiveness is not synonymous with weakness in any way. Being submissive to the male leaders of the church does not mean that women are second-class to men. None of this means women aren't capable of serving in the church.

Look at the work done by the women in the first century. In Romans 16, Paul commends many women—Phoebe, Priscilla, Mary, Tryphena, Tryphosa, Persis, Rufus' mother, Julia, and others. None of them had special titles and were simply referred to as workers. It is possible to work for the Lord—for all the wrong reasons—if we let self-importance, recognition, status, and titles get in the way. As simply workers for the Lord, we can be assured that the Lord is pleased with our service as we humbly submit to His will.

What Can We Do?

Sometimes we get the idea that if we cannot be an official spiritual leader with a title, we have no value at all. At other times, we get the idea that male spiritual leadership means that women are not to be educated in the Scripture, or that, if we are, we are to keep it to ourselves. Not true! There are many things that educated Christian women can do to serve.

We can encourage the leaders of the congregation in whatever endeavor they undertake. We can encourage the mothers to bring up their children in the ways of the Lord. What better way to work for the Lord than to be hospitable to others and to be service oriented? We can be helpful to those who are in trouble; we can be good examples of a Christian woman, devoted to all kinds of good works.

Young women, you can make an impact in all areas of Christian service. Ask a friend to study the Bible with you and don't hesitate to invite a seasoned personal worker to assist. Invite a friend to worship, youth meetings, and ladies' days; be an example of faithful attendance. Volunteer to help the needy by working in the church pantry. Team up with another Christian and send notes to the weak and the strong. Learn to bake communion bread and assist in preparing the Lord's supper. Join with an older Christian and visit the sick and elderly.

Attitudes

A good, humble attitude goes a long way in accepting the teachings of the Bible concerning the role of women in public worship.

Although the concept of male spiritual leadership is taught, nothing is less Christ-like than for one to act as a know-it-all in all matters.

The role of women in public worship and the study of customs in the first century are challenging and sometimes controversial issues. We can be respectful of other's opinions, and we must avoid getting into meaningless and unscriptural arguments—if they are truly matters of opinion. In matters of the truth, we must remain strong in our convictions and uphold the teachings of the Bible, even when considered old fashioned by today's standards—and this truth must be taught in love. Without it more harm than good can result.

Men and women are truly equal in God's eyes, but we have different roles. With that thought in mind, the concept of submission by women can be approached with acceptance and joy, rather than confusion and frustration.

It's Your Turn!

1. In what ways do feminism and Christianity clash?

2. In what ways can a Christian woman support feminism—or can she?

3. Read 1 Timothy 2:14. Does this verse explain why woman may have lost any leadership position she may have had in the Garden of Eden?

4. Compare the Virtuous Woman portrayed in Proverbs 31 to radical feminists.

5. Explain Paul's statement that "women are to keep silent" in the church (1 Corinthians 14:34).

6. What are some ways a Christian woman can serve in the Lord's church?

7. What does the Bible teach about woman's qualifications to serve as a deacon or an elder?

8. Would there be anything wrong with a woman teaching a mixed-gender class of Christians, if the elders gave her permission? Why or why not?

9. How can a Christian woman be both submissive and independent?

10. Does being tolerant of another person's viewpoints about women's roles mean you have no convictions of your own? Why or why not?

CHAPTER TWELVE

This Is My Life!
Compromising Our Stewardship

Fence-Straddling Position: "Surely you don't expect me to give up my money, too! This is mine, Lord. I earned it."

Bible Position: "And He said to them, Take heed and beware of covetousness, for one's life does not consist in the abundance of the things he possesses" (Luke 12:15).

Scripture Search

Psalms 49
Proverbs 23:4–5
Ecclesiastes 5:10; 15–17
Malachi 3:8–10
Matthew 6:19–21
Matthew 16:26
Mark 8:36
Mark 12:41–44

Luke 12:15–21
Acts 20:35
1 Corinthians 16:1–2
2 Corinthians 9:6–7
Philippians 4:11–13
Colossians 3:5
1 Timothy 6:6–10
Hebrews 13:5

Say What?

Steward—One who manages another's financial affairs or property.

Materialism—Attention to or emphasis on material objects, needs, and considerations, with a disinterest in or rejection of spiritual values.

Greed—Extreme desire for something, often more than one's share, and many times for wealth.

Covetousness—Greediness.

Contentment—Satisfaction; happiness.

Idolatry—The worship of a tangible or intangible object, such as money, status, or power.

Perdition—Spiritual ruin.

Vanity—Something vain, empty, or useless. Inflated pride in oneself or one's appearance.

Tithe—To pay or give one-tenth of one's income.

Purpose—Resolve, plan, intention.

Lisa eyed the new car her friend Britney had received for her sixteenth birthday. What a beauty! *she thought.* What I wouldn't give to have that.

It wasn't just any car either—it was new, it was sporty, and it was a BMW. Why does Britney have all the luck? *thought Lisa as she slipped into her old clunker.* She doesn't even appreciate it, either. Her family gives her anything she wants . . .

Lisa was lost in her own covetous thoughts when Britney suddenly tapped on her window. "Hey, Lisa—you want to take a ride in my new car? I'm going over to the mall and thought you might like to join me."

"Sure," said Lisa. "I was just heading out there myself."

Besides, *Lisa thought to herself,* now maybe someone will see me in this nice machine instead of that old thing I'm driving.

As they drove toward the mall in the shiny, new car, Lisa began, "This is great! Britney, you don't know how lucky you are. Your parents are super—and have great taste, I might add!"

Britney just smiled, as she seemed lost in her own thoughts. "Lisa, you know, you may think I've lost it here, but I think your parents are the ones that are super," she said slowly.

"What?" Lisa was dumbfounded. "Why in the world would you think that?"

"Now, don't get me wrong. I love this car, and I love my parents for what they think they are giving me," Britney said slowly. "But you know what? I almost never see them, and when I do, they are always so busy and in such a hurry. I get all the money I want, but I don't get any of their time. Does that seem silly to you?"

"Well, you've always seemed to have it made," stammered Lisa. "Look at your clothes, your house, and now this car. Lots of people would die for all this . . ."

"Yeah, but listen to what I'm trying to say," Britney continued. "Remember the time your parents took us to their old homeplace and showed us how they used to live? Remember the cookouts in your backyard? The ballgames? Remember how all our friends loved to come to your house?"

"Well, yes, of course, I remember all those things," Lisa said. "So what? I still don't have a BMW!" she laughed. "You're still the lucky one. Your parents will buy you anything you want."

"Yeah, you've got that part right. They will buy me anything I want, but I don't remember the last time we did anything together. I'm just sick of the whole thing. Don't get me wrong—I love them, I just wish things were a little different."

"I guess I never thought of it that way." Suddenly Lisa was ashamed of herself. Britney had a point.

"You're the lucky one, Lisa, not me," Britney said as she parked the car. Don't you ever forget that . . ."

I, too, am quite fond of the car I drive. On the driver's side window of my car is a little sticker with a funny face on it that simply says, "Life is Good." Indeed, life *is* good.

I hope no one would ever misunderstand my intent in placing that sticker on my window. In no way was it meant to be boastful or arrogant about anything I possess. But I loved that saying when I first heard it. It symbolizes the goodness, the blessings, and the abundance so many of us enjoy today. On the other hand, maybe life has become too good.

Day after day we are encouraged the think about material things. The last decade of the twentieth century was the longest run of prosperity in history with the stock market boom, low unemployment rates, and good, easy money in general. We are bombarded daily with advertisements and enticements that we should find the jobs that pay the most money, invest in the stock market, strengthen our financial portfolios, and plan our retirement.

Planning for our future is one thing; hoarding up riches on earth and trusting in them is another. In Matthew 6:19–21, Jesus tells us not to lay up treasures on earth, but rather to lay up treasures in Heaven. How many times have we quoted those scriptures? But how many really believe their message? We can understand plainly what Jesus is saying, yet they are some of the hardest scriptures to put into practice.

We have much more than we need today, especially in America, yet we are often consumed by greed and desire. Christmas is truly a joyous occasion with my large family, but oh, the piles of gifts we go through each year! Are all these material gifts necessary? Of course, not!

My family is probably not much different from many others in that regard. We all have so much it seems as though we are unfeeling sometimes. We have come to feel that we deserve these things—just because. But are we satisfied? Before we can ever be satisfied or content, we must learn to appreciate what we have and what has been done for us. If we learn to really appreciate what we have and be thankful for our blessings and all that has been given to us, we will truly be content.

Contentment

What is contentment? Happiness resulting from satisfaction with what we have. The dictionary defines it as "feeling satisfaction with one's possessions, status or situation." Paul said in

Philippians 4:11 that he had learned to be satisfied or contented with the things he had and with everything that happened!

He explains it even further in 1 Timothy 6:7–10 when he says:

> For we brought nothing into this world, and it is certain that we can carry nothing out. And having food and clothing, with these we shall be content. But those who desire to be rich fall into temptation and a snare, and into many foolish and harmful lusts which drown men in destruction and perdition. For the love of money is a root of all kinds of evil, for which some have strayed from the faith in their greediness, and pierced themselves through with many sorrows.

First Timothy 6:6 is an often-quoted scripture that shows us where our emphasis should lie: "Godliness with contentment is great gain."

Contentment is the evidence of our faith that we know God will provide all our needs in the time that is right and good. When we truly understand what God has done and continues to do for us, we will be content with what we have in life, and this contentment will release us from the rat race of materialism. Contentment is not found in having everything our hearts desire, but in being satisfied with everything we do have.

Does this mean it's wrong to be ambitious or to want material things? No. There's nothing wrong with having money or things— as long as those material things do not become idols to us. Where's our trust? Is it in God or in our own ability to make money?

It All Starts with Money

In the Gospel accounts, Jesus Christ talked about money and material possessions more than anything else. Sixteen of Christ's 38 parables speak about how people should handle earthly treasures. John MacArthur, in his book, *Whose Money Is It, Anyway?* gives this account:

> The Lord taught more about such stewardship (one out of every ten verses in the Gospels) than about heaven and hell combined. The entire Bible contains more than two thousand references to wealth and property, twice as many as the total references to faith and prayer. What we do with the things God has given us is very important to Him.

There is a mistaken idea that the money we earn is truly our money. Sure, we go out and earn it through our jobs, and we work hard to have the necessities and all our nice things. But the money is not actually ours at all. It is a rare individual today who really understands this. All our blessings, including money and material things, are from God and belong to Him.

If we Christians have the right attitude toward money and will honestly give of our means back to God, we are well on our way to being the Christian steward God wants. It truly all starts with money and our attitude toward it. Hasn't God promised to take care of us? Jesus told us in Matthew 6:25:

> Do not worry about your life, what you will eat or what you will drink; nor about your body, what you will put on. Is not life more than food and the body more than clothing?

Our faith is tragically weak in this regard.

What Is a Steward?

A steward is one who is trusted to take care of another's property or financial affairs. We usually think of stewardship as managing money, but we as Christians must properly handle all the blessings God has put in our care. Consider the following blessings and determine to be a good steward in each.

- *Give Our Treasure.* Will we continue to drop a dollar in the collection plate each Sunday, as we did when we were children, and be done with our contribution for another week? To be a good steward, we must examine our giving to the Lord and to the church and its good deeds.

  The Jews were required to give a tithe, or at least one-tenth of what they earned to the Lord. Although tithing is not specifically commanded in the New Testament, Christians should use the tithe as a starting point for determining how much we should give to the church today. Should we give any less than the Jews did in their day? Surely not.

- *Give Our Time.* With only a short time allotted for our lives, we should be constantly aware of the passing of our days. How do we spend our time? Will we watch another mindless TV show? Will we squander our time by doing only what we want to do? What a tragedy to waste our opportunities to serve others and bring souls to Christ.

  When you budget your time, remember to make a sincere effort to spend some of it with those who are lonely or in trouble. And don't forget your own family members. Sometimes in our attempts to do good deeds, even for the church, we become bogged down and forget those who are closest to us. We should also never forget to take time to talk to God.

• *Give our Talents.* In addition to our material possessions, our money, and our time, God has also blessed every one of us with individual talents. Fight the temptation to hide or bury your talents, and pay special attention not to misuse them! What better way to serve Him than to develop our talents further for His glory?

The Lure of Materialism

Materialism is "the attention to or emphasis on material (physical, worldly) objects, needs, and considerations, with a disinterest in or rejection of spiritual values." It is just another word for greed. God looks upon greed as harshly as He does on what we sometimes incorrectly think of as the "major sins" such as adultery and murder. Greed is always motivated by selfishness.

Ephesians 5:5 says emphatically: "For this you know, that no fornicator, unclean person, nor covetous man, who is an idolater, has any inheritance in the kingdom of Christ and God."

First Corinthians 6:9–10 lists greedy people alongside adulterers, homosexuals, drunkards, robbers, and liars. Colossians 3:5–6 says:

> Therefore put to death your members which are on the earth: fornication, uncleanness, passion, evil desire, and covetousness, which is idolatry. Because of these things the wrath of God is coming upon the sons of disobedience.

These verses should definitely get our attention!

Some are saying materialism is the most serious problem facing the church today—not as a philosophical theory, but as a way of life. George Barna, a well-known researcher of American values, says that even though materialism has received a bad rap from both the press and from the Christian community, it still continues to rule the minds and hearts of Americans. By nature we are greedy and often forget that God is the giver and owner of all our material treasures.

It is easy to be lured into wanting more and more—or just wanting our fair share. What is the harm? Although it is not sinful to have money and possessions, it is definitely sinful to hoard, worship, and covet them as symbols of prestige, and overindulge by building our lives around them. Paul said the love of money is the root of all kinds of evil (1 Timothy 6:10).

Solomon, one of the richest, yet wisest kings of the world, taught many practical lessons. Among his best are the lessons and guidelines from the book of Ecclesiastes. Like many who lived before him and those who lived after him, Solomon searched for the meaning of life. He tried everything under the sun in his pursuit of happiness and the meaning of life. He decided to pursue all his heart desired. He had women, great wealth, wisdom, and power. In Ecclesiastes 2:10–11, Solomon said:

> Whatever my eyes desired I did not keep from them. I did not withhold my heart from any pleasure, for my heart rejoiced in all my labor; and this was my reward from all my labor. Then I looked on all the works that my hands had done and on the labor in which I had toiled; and indeed all was vanity and grasping for the wind. There was no profit under the sun.

How many of us today continue to search for happiness, as Solomon did, through our relentless pursuit of things and our continuing to chase the wind? In the final chapter of Ecclesiastes, Solomon concluded two major lessons from his search for the meaning of life: (1) it's better to be content with what little we have, or otherwise, we will always be struggling for more; and (2) our whole duty on this earth is to fear God and keep his commandments.

Materialism—A Women's Issue?

While this book deals with special problems and issues pertaining to young Christian women today, materialism is not usually automatically presumed to be a women's issue. However, this is an issue that should be addressed by each young Christian woman.

Women can certainly be lured as easily as men when it comes to acquiring things, wanting things we really don't need, and having to have only the best. Sadly, women represent a majority when it comes to vanity purchases—cosmetics, clothes, and personal items. In and of themselves, these things are not sinful, but we need to be on guard to keep these gadgets and vanity purchases from becoming gods to us. Our priorities should remain solidly on God—not on the world.

Women must also understand that the commandment to give in 1 Corinthians 16:1–2 is not directed only to men. We are responsible, too. Paul said in verse 2: "On the first day of the week let *each one of you* lay something aside, storing up as he may prosper, that there be no collections when I come."

Many women work outside the home today or will work at a job some time in their lives. We need to give back to the Lord—liberally, cheerfully, and sacrificially. Even a stay-at-home mom who isn't bringing in any money can still give of her time and talents to the Lord. She can also become a good steward by managing her household finances well and learning to be thrifty, so her family can give liberally to the church and to the Lord.

The Arrogance of Possessing the Best

Mr. Barna also says his research has shown that Americans, having failed to satisfy themselves through possessing more, are now seeking to satisfy themselves by possessing the best. It's no longer satisfying to have everything our hearts desire, we now want the name brands, the biggest, the latest, and only the best.

"Trophy travel" is the latest craze for travelers wishing to impress others with their exotic vacations. No longer is it impressive and dramatic enough to just go on a vacation. Many are now booking vacations and paying exorbitant prices to visit remote and expensive locales, often for no other reason than to impress others with their money and their sophistication in world travel.

Another example that comes to mind is the silliness of owning the best athletic shoes. Some teenagers have even killed others to steal their shoes! It has become shameful for them to wear anything but brand-name athletic shoes. Just a few years ago, Reebok offered 175 different models of athletic shoes in 450 colors. Not to be outdone, Nike offered over 300 models and 900 colors! What are we thinking?

Of course, it's not just shoes or vacations. Our arrogance is seen in many of our other possessions—only the best cell phones, electronic gadgets, sunglasses, beepers, and cars will do. Where are our priorities? What is really important to us any more? Money does indeed buy things, but can money buy peace, love, joy, or salvation? We must make a stand quickly and decisively by making better choices about how we spend our money.

Some Practical Ways to Think about Money

The following are some common-sense ways for us to avoid straddling the fence in our attitudes toward money and to help in our study of stewardship. Consider these practical ways to think about money.

- *Give Ourselves to the Lord.* It's insulting to give our scraps to God. From the beginning of time, He has always looked harshly on those who did not give of their first fruits. We must first give our lives to God, and then we can cheerfully give back to Him and give to others (2 Corinthians 8:5). Matthew 6:33 says we will truly be rewarded if we seek Him first.

- *Learn to Manage Money Well.* Numerous classes dealing with budgeting and managing money are now available through the Internet, colleges, and community classes. Many times we get into trouble with credit cards and free-spirited spending because we are accustomed to instant gratification. It might not be easy; it might be what others seem to be doing. But in the long run, budgeting and spending wisely will pay off, both financially and in peace of mind.

  It is important for you to develop a plan of giving back to the Lord while you are young. Giving is not optional. God has commanded that we give of our means just as He has commanded us to believe on Him and to be baptized. We must plan our giving and we must give cheerfully.

- *Learn to Live Within Our Means.* One of the most important lessons a young Christian women can learn is to live within her means. If we don't get a handle on our spending, we are headed for days of financial troubles, depression, anxiety, and worry. We should make a commitment to learn how to save and to avoid the instant gratification mindset so prevalent in today's society.

- *Be Thrifty Without Being Stingy.* God wants and expects us to be generous. No one likes a woman who is stingy or self-centered. Even Christians of average means can be stingy; it's all about our attitude. We need to make a commitment to give generously to the church and to others—and to start at a young age.

- *We Can't Take It with Us.* We should enjoy what we have and be forever thankful to God for supplying whatever we have. Christians should never hoard their money, but be willing to share with others. We brought nothing into the world and can take nothing with us when we die.

Red Flags Concerning Money

How can we tell if we have the proper attitude toward money? John MacArthur discusses some ways we could display the wrong attitude toward money. These red flags, as he calls them, are caution marks for us to use to determine if we are having problems with money. He states:

> A lover of money will be bent on making money any way possible, they never seem to have enough money, they will most likely flaunt it and brag about it, and they usually hate to give to others.

Those four warnings can serve as red flags to all of us concerning our attitudes toward money.

God As Number One

Knowing that God owns all we have and is the giver of all we have, we should always strive to keep Him number one in our lives. Simply, the Lord will not settle for second place. When we let money become our greatest love and passion, then money becomes a god to us.

Keeping our priorities in order concerning stewardship will help us avoid straddling the fence when it comes to making decisions about managing our finances. Remember, money is not evil, having possessions is not wrong, having a good job is an admirable goal, but our priorities must remain in order. It is truly the love of money and the relentless pursuit of it that will get us in trouble. Pray to God for guidance and wisdom in determining His plan for your stewardship.

It's Your Turn!

1. What is a modern-day definition of a steward?

2. What are some ways one can plan and save for retirement years without hoarding their money?

3. Why do you think the Gospel accounts have more of Jesus' teaching on money than on any other subject?

4. What are some ways we can be good stewards, other than having a good attitude about money and giving our money to the Lord?

5. Is it possible to be contented and still have ambition? How?

6. Why do you think Paul said in Philippians 4:11 that he had learned to be content in all things?

7. Is investing in the stock market a form of gambling? Why or why not?

8. How much money should a Christian give back to the Lord? Is tithing required today?

9. How can possessions or money make us proud?

10. What are some practical ways to avoid materialism?

CHAPTER THIRTEEN

Been There, Done That: Lessons Learned

Compromising Our Christianity

Fence-Straddling Position: "You may have forgiven me, God, but I can never forgive myself. I've done too much wrong to ever come back to the church, I could never change, and I would never fit it. It's hopeless."

Bible Position: "Come to Me, all you who labor and are heavy laden, and I will give you rest. Take My yoke upon you and learn from Me, for I am gentle and lowly in heart, and you will find rest for your souls. For My yoke is easy and My burden is light" (Matthew 11:28-30).

Scripture Search

Isaiah 5:21   Proverbs 14:12
Psalms 37:3-7   Proverbs 16:2
Psalms 103:12   Luke 15:11–32
Proverbs 12:15   1 Corinthians 3:18–19
1 Timothy 4:12

Say What?

Compromise—To make a shameful concession. Yielding. Blending with others. Middle ground.

Apathy—Indifference; lack of interest or concern. Lack of feelings or emotions.

Guilt—A feeling of responsibility or remorse for some real or imagined offense.

Forgive—To grant free pardon for or remission of an offense. To stop feeling resentment against someone for some offense done toward you or others.

Peace—Freedom of the mind from unrest, annoyances, and strife. Tranquility, stillness.

Unconditional Love—Love given to another without limits, conditions, or restrictions, such as love of a parent for a child or the love of God for all mankind.

Repent—To feel sorry for a past action and to turn away from it.

Consequences—Results.

Priorities—The order of importance we place on certain things or activities in our life.

Balance—State of stability or harmony.

Who is this Bozo? *Seventeen-year-old Jennifer squirmed in her seat wishing she were anywhere but at a Christian girls' youth rally listening to an old lady trying to turn fun things into sin. But it was either be here or not spend the night with Joni next Friday. And they were going to have fun!*

"I never meant for my life to turn out exactly as it did." *The speaker was Melissa, a 30-year-old alcoholic divorcee.* "I was asked to speak to you today, not because of some great accomplishment I have achieved and neither because I am some inherently evil person. But hopefully, you can gain a little something from my short speech. A few short years ago, I was just like you, and today I will *share my story about how chipping away my Christian beliefs turned my life into one of uncertainty, confusion, deception, and depression. I want to talk to you today about compromise and apathy."*

Jennifer groaned within herself: Just another old lady telling me all the stuff she's been through and blah, blah, blah . . .

But some of the girls were captivated by Melissa's sincerity: "I've sat in audiences like you are in today. Like many of you, I was raised in the church. I knew I'd been blessed with a good life. At one time, I had a good marriage, a comfortable home, a secure and profitable job, good health, and all the toys one could ever want. In so many ways, I had it made. But I lost all those things when I compromised my beliefs—slowly one at a time until I had virtually nothing left.

"Nothing bad happened overnight, since compromise is usually a slow process that becomes more destructive over time. What difference did one drink make? So I began to drink. It wasn't long until I was experimenting with drugs, and every weekend became a party. But something else was wrong—something was missing. That missing link, I knew, was peace.

"The restlessness that stayed with me for many years had a lot to do with my trying to be a Christian on Sunday and just like the world the rest of the week. I was essentially a Sunday-morning Christian. Roots that shallow are bound to eventually be uprooted.

"On the outside, my life appeared to be on the right track, but inside I had made so many compromises that my life bore little resemblance of a Christian—especially to my worldly friends. I was just like them.

" 'How did this happen?' was the question that stayed in my head day and night.

"The answer hit me like a ton of bricks, although it shouldn't have been such a surprise. I woke up to the fact that I had basically compromised every Christian principle I had ever stood for until I no longer had any strong convictions about anything. Since I never took a stand one way or the other, I became so apathetic I didn't care if you or I drank, used drugs, cursed, practiced homosexuality, was promiscuous, wore immodest clothing, favored abortion, supported radical feminism, or if women preached in our pulpits. I was simply neutral."

Jennifer leaned forward as Melissa continued: "Because of compromise, I lost my marriage, my self-respect, my sobriety, and much peace of mind. What seemed like small concessions on meaningless subjects ended up being just one more example of a little chip, chip, chipping away—until there was nothing left of me or my Christianity. I didn't care anymore."

Whatever else Melissa said was lost to Jennifer. At those words, she sat up straight and suddenly felt her cheeks grow hot. She knew exactly what Melissa was talking about! Hadn't it been just last month she'd taken a drink—just a tiny little wine cooler. Hadn't she made a decision to skip church a lot lately—but it was just on Sunday and Wednesday nights? It felt a little weird at first, but now she didn't even think about it much. What difference did it make if she cheated on her final—it was only once and she'd been so good all year. She had smoked a little pot this year, but at least she didn't go out and get drunk every weekend. And next Friday night at Joni's house, with Joni's parents away on vacation—of course Keith would be there! She and Keith were getting closer in their relationship. Nearly everyone she knew had already had sex . . . Surely, nothing bad would come of these little decisions . . . Surely not . . .

Suddenly, Jennifer bolted from her daydreaming. Melissa was finishing her speech with the bold statement, "If you remember nothing else from this talk today, please remember the words com-promise and apathy. They're both killers. As young Christian women, stand for something—or you'll fall for anything. Better yet, stand up for what's right. Little things do count!"

Compromise and *apathy* are two of the most dangerous words in a Christian woman's vocabulary. Either characteristic is destructive enough alone, but putting the two together is a sure way to lose all influence, the desire to do right, and peace of mind.

Perhaps you can relate to some of the concessions Melissa and Jennifer made, as I surely can. Many times, we find ourselves caught somewhere in the middle ground of compromise. The realization that you are indeed there can quietly appear on your conscience one day or slap you suddenly from an apathetic stupor. In any case, it almost always leads us to change.

From my own years of compromise, I would like to share a few personal thoughts in this final chapter. This chapter is written to all the good, young Christian women who may stumble in their Christianity or waver in their faith—and to those who just want to go home again. Take it from one, who like Melissa, has truly "been there, done that."

The Scars of Sin

I have an ugly scar on my left shoulder. It's the result of surgery performed to repair an injury brought on by years of playing sports. For some reason, this incision didn't heal properly and now I am left with the scar.

More importantly, I also have several scars on my heart—not my physical heart, of course, but my soul. Those scars take time to heal, too. Sometimes, I'm afraid they never do completely heal.

Just as the scar on my shoulder reminds me of physical mistakes I made, the scars on my heart continually remind me of the mistakes I've made otherwise in my life. The scars of sin are hard to erase. If there is one point I wish to leave any young reader in this closing chapter, it is this thought: there are consequences of sin.

Unfortunately, there are also consequences for poor decision-making. Seemingly trivial decisions you make today could affect the course of your entire life. Making good choices is really that important. Of course, God can and does forgive when we mess up. Nothing is too big or too bad for God to forgive, but forgiving ourselves is another matter entirely. Often those scars on our hearts fester and continue to bleed for years, and constantly remind us of our mistakes.

Forgiving Ourselves

Jesus said in Matthew 6:14–15 that we must forgive those who sin against us or else God will not forgive us of our sins. Although it is sometimes extremely difficult to forgive others for doing something wrong or hurtful toward us, most of us do try hard to forgive others and most of the times we are successful.

But when it comes to forgiving ourselves, it is an altogether different story. We are often very hard on ourselves. Why is it so hard to forgive ourselves after we repent and God has forgiven us and forgotten about it?

Many of us feel unworthy of God's forgiveness. We think we are "too bad" or have done something that is unforgivable. The blood of Christ is powerful, though, and will cleanse us of any sin we will confess and turn from. Notice the list of sins Paul mentioned in 1 Corinthians 6:9–11, including adultery, murder, and homosexuality. Some of the Corinthians had been guilty of those sins before their conversion to Christ, but by His blood they were cleansed, and had been washed, sanctified, and justified in the name of the Lord Jesus. If a person is unwilling to acknowledge and repent of a certain sin and is determined to "take it to her grave," that sin does become one God will not forgive. How can He forgive it if we won't acknowledge it and turn from it?

Another reason we can't forgive ourselves is that guilt won't leave us alone. Although we may have repented and thought our sin was out of our minds, Satan likes to bring up the past over and over again. We may also feel remorseful and a bit foolish for some of the choices we have made, so we constantly berate ourselves.

The biggest reason it is so hard to forgive ourselves, though, goes back to the consequences of sin. Many times, we live with the result of our sins and our choices for the rest of our lives; consequently, it's hard to ever forget about them, so we don't forgive ourselves.

An alcoholic might eventually put away the alcohol and be forgiven by God. But she might have destroyed her body and family in the process. A woman might divorce, but the thoughts of her former life and what might have been may never completely leave her mind. A young lady who becomes pregnant and has an abortion will go on and live her life, but the anguish and guilt of aborting her child might never leave her heart. So the guilt continues and forgiving ourselves becomes harder to do.

However, we must remind ourselves as Christians that God our Father always stands ready to receive us back home and forgive us when we repent and confess our sins to Him. Then He forgets it. David was constantly reminded of his sin of adultery with Bathsheba and the subsequent murder of her husband. If ever there was a remorseful person, it was David. Hear his confession as he prays: "For I acknowledge my transgressions, and my sin is always before me. Against You, You only, have I sinned, and done this evil in Your sight" (Psalms 51:3–4).

Even the great apostle Paul felt remorse and guilt when he remembered his former life. Since he had persecuted and killed Christians, he said in 1 Timothy 1:15 that Jesus had come into the world to save sinners of whom he was the chief or worst.

It may take time and practice for us to learn to forgive ourselves. In Psalms 103:12, David tells us of the incredible way in which God forgives and then forgets: "As far as the east is from the west, so far has He removed our transgressions from us." Remember, God loves us and will forgive when we ask forgiveness and turn from our sins. Once we truly understand and accept God's forgiveness, we can forgive ourselves. We need to forgive ourselves after repenting of our sins—God has. We need to get on with our lives!

Lessons Learned

Often I'm reminded of an expression that was common in my workplace as a federal employee supporting the soldiers in the war during Operation Desert Storm. Working closely in the logistical area providing the troops with supplies, ammunition, technical support, and equipment, my group had to be ready to answer our superiors quickly on how we could improve our processes. What could we have done differently or how could we have made things work better or more smoothly to support the troops? Those replies were consolidated into reports we affectionately called "Lessons Learned."

In closing this study, I too would like to offer some practical lessons I've learned during my life, all derived from a scripture in the Bible that has made an impact on me. Hopefully, these lessons learned from my own life will help you as a young Christian woman avoid straddling the fence on controversial issues, but even more importantly, help you to thrive in your life as a Christian woman. The following are a few of my favorites. Enjoy!

To Avoid Straddling the Fence:

- *Take Time to Be Holy.* "Study to show thyself approved unto God, a workman that needeth not to be ashamed, rightly dividing the word of God" (2 Timothy 2:15). To be holy in thought and deed, take time to study God's Word. Don't just read it, but be a student of the Bible. Christ changes people, and the

Bible can literally change your life. Knowing what the scriptures teach is the best way to avoid straddling the fence.

- *Develop a Good Prayer Life*. "Be anxious for nothing, but in everything by prayer and supplications, with thanksgiving, let your requests be known to God, and the peace which surpasses all understanding will guard your hearts and minds through Christ Jesus" (Philippians 4:6–7). So often, we say we will pray for this or that or we'll pray for someone, but do we mean it? What a shame to waste this avenue and great privilege we have to talk to our Father. God has promised to hear our prayers. Pray often—and pray boldly with all confidence.

- *Choose Friends Wisely*. "Do not be deceived: evil company corrupts good habits" (1 Corinthians 15:33). Everyone wants to be liked and accepted by her peers. Friends must be chosen carefully, though, and it is important to surround yourself with people of character and conviction. While appreciating others and their opinions, you must make a decision that you will not blindly follow your friends in every endeavor they undertake. The wrong friends can take you away from God. It may not seem to matter, but consider this thought that has always left an impression on me, no matter how many times I heard it: "Sin took me farther than I intended to go, cost me more than I meant to pay, and kept me longer than I ever thought I would stay." Evil companions can lead you into sin.

- *Set Priorities*. "But seek first the kingdom of God and His righteousness, and all these things shall be added to you" (Matthew 6:33). From studying the Bible, decide while you're young what is important in your life. Decide what things can be omitted. Make it a priority to marry a Christian. Try not to get caught up in the materialism of the world. Seek Christ first. Remember to set your standards high and establish some meaningful goals. Not knowing what your priorities are is a sure way to back down in times of controversy.

- *Just Do It*. "He is a double-minded man, unstable in all his ways" (James 1:8). Impulsiveness can lead to many bad decisions. On the other hand, you as a young woman will have to make many decisions in your life. Learn to make a decision, and don't be afraid of making a mistake. If you are swayed to and fro by every possible argument and try to please everyone all the time, you are sure to lose your confidence and ability to think reasonably. Knowing what God wants and expects of you makes it easier for you to stand on your own two feet and make a Christ-centered decision. When faced with an important decision, make a list of pros and cons, pray to God for guidance in making the best choice, then just do it—make a decision and stick to it.

- *Accept Responsibility for Your Actions.* "But if you do not do so, then take note, you have sinned against the Lord, and be sure your sin will find you out" (Numbers 32:23). It's human nature to look for someone else to blame for your actions or mistakes— parents, friends, or even God. But ultimately you are responsible for your own decisions and choices. There will always be consequences for those choices, either good or bad. Accepting bad decisions, repenting of your sins, and asking God's help in overcoming them are the most important lessons learned in becoming a mature Christian.

- *Get Rid of the Clutter.* "Let us lay aside every weight, and the sin which so easily ensnares us, and let us run with endurance the race that is set before us, looking to Jesus, the author and finisher of our faith" (Hebrews 12:1–2). In today's world, you'll find it easy to let your life become cluttered. It may not necessarily be sin that will entangle you so much as your life just becomes too cluttered. You may be guilty of having "too many irons in the fire." Life can become burdensome with too much to do. You may be guilty of simply having too many things and your life may become cluttered with possessions, rather than good deeds that are befitting a Christian. Make sure that all the stuff you acquire is not about filling a void in your soul. Clutter and acquiring things can keep you from being all you can be for Christ and can cause you to compromise your faith for material things.

- *Grow Up.* "Add to your faith virtue, to virtue knowledge, to knowledge self-control, to self-control perseverance, to perseverance godliness, to godliness brotherly kindness, and to brotherly kindness love" (2 Peter 1:5–7). Just as a baby must grow up to be an adult, so must you grow up as a Christian. Peter tells how to do that in the above passage. Make a commitment to practice those traits in becoming the mature Christian woman you should be.

- *Be True to Yourself.* "Remember now your Creator in the days of your youth, before the difficult days come, and the years draw near when you say, 'I have no pleasure in them'" (Ecclesiastes 12:1). Most of the time Christians know deep down what is right and what is wrong since we have been taught and understand the concepts of morality and biblical principles. Even though you may be tempted at times to say you don't understand why you aren't as close to the Lord as you should be, you usually know the reason. A preacher once illustrated it this way: A young woman kept insisting she didn't know what was keeping her from being close to the Lord and she didn't know what to repent of. The preacher told her, "Get on your knees and guess!" Point being, you usually know what is keeping you from the Lord. Be true to yourself.

- *Trust in the Lord.* "Trust in the Lord with all your heart, and lean not on your own understanding; in all your ways acknowledge Him, and He shall direct your paths" (Proverbs 3:5–6). Learn to walk that fine line of being able to use your God-given ability to make decisions, without totally trusting or leaning on yourself to make all your decisions. God knows what you need and you should be willing to bring your problems to the Lord and pray for wisdom in making good decisions. He will truly protect you and guide you in all you do.

To Live Happy for the Rest of Your Life:

- *Be Contented.* "For I have learned in whatever state I am, to be content" (Philippians 4:11). It's so easy to look around at our friends and neighbors and be discontented with our lot in life. So for a happier life, avoid the comparison game at all costs. Someone will always have a nicer car, a bigger house, a better job, and more money. Remember that Paul said he had *learned* to be content—we will have to put some effort into learning to be content with our lives. There is nothing wrong with being ambitious and making your life all it can be, but beware of dissatisfaction with your possessions. Seize the day and be happy and contented with whatever stage of life you find yourself—enjoy being a young person without wishing your life away—enjoy your college days, enjoy your working days, or your days at home with your children. Don't put off your happiness until "some day" in the future. God wants you to enjoy this wonderful life He has blessed you with. Smile, rejoice in the Lord, and be contented. Enjoy life!

- *Learn to Forgive.* "Judge not, and you shall not be judged. Condemn not, and you shall not be condemned. Forgive, and you will be forgiven" (Luke 6:37). Not forgiving others when they do something against you is a sure way to poison your life. I've seen the lives of some of my friends ruined simply because they could not forgive another. Spite and resentment will build up when you don't forgive someone, and you will most likely end up hurting yourself more than the other person. Of course, to be truly happy, you must also forgive yourself when you make mistakes.

- *Esteem Others Better Than Yourself.* "Let nothing be done through selfish ambition or conceit, but in lowliness of mind let each esteem others better than himself. Let each of you look out not only for his own interests, but also for the interests of others" (Philippians 2:3–4). In other words, be humble and honor others more than yourself. Remember to be interested in the lives of other people, not only in your own life. You can do this by listening to others instead of doing all the talking. Focusing on others will help you not to think about yourself so much and will bring joy and happiness to yourself, as well as to others.

- *Consider the Lilies of the Field.* "Consider the lilies of the field, how they grow: they neither toil nor spin; and yet I say to you that even Solomon in all his glory was not arrayed like one of these" (Matthew 6:28–29). Don't have so little faith, and don't worry about the clothes you need to wear or the food you need to eat. God will take care of you! Also remember that Jesus said to seek first the kingdom of heaven and all these earthly necessities would be provided. Take time to look at the world in which you live and appreciate nature and this beautiful world God created and gave to you.

- *Develop a Good Sense of Humor.* "A merry heart makes a cheerful countenance" (Proverbs 15:13). To make life all it can be and should be, learn to have fun and enjoy life by being with friends and family, sharing good times, and laughing. Learning to laugh at yourself will ease the frustrations and disappointments of life and the mistakes that you will make along the way. Look for the bright side, and don't take yourself too seriously.

- *Get a Life.* "For what is your life? It is even a vapor that appears for a little time and then vanishes away" (James 4:14). Time and again in the Bible, we are reminded of the shortness of life. Make up your mind to enjoy your life by making each moment count. Be involved in living life to its fullest, and care about something! Don't be afraid of a little work! While it is nice to have others to lean on, life will be a little simpler if you will learn some practical things for yourself. Learn to change a tire, mow the yard, fix a toilet! Glamorous? Hardly. However, you may be forced to take care of yourself at sometime in your life, and if you can learn to do a few things on your own, life will not be so frustrating. Taking care of little problems and challenges that come your way is a good way to build self-confidence.

- *Find Your Niche.* "For as we have many members in one body, but all the members do not have the same function, so we, being many, are one body in Christ, and individually members of one another" (Romans 12:4–5). Thankfully, no two people are exactly alike! We all have different interests, talents, and abilities. It is important to find where you fit in—whether it be at your job, with your family, or in the church. The church especially needs to be aware of the ever-changing demographic makeup of congregations today. Families are important, but so are single, divorced, young, and old people. As a young Christian woman, find your niche, and be aware it will change over time as you change. Be willing to ask what you can do to serve others.

- *Don't Forget You're a Woman.* "Then the rib which the Lord God had taken from man He made into a woman, and He brought her to the man" (Genesis 2:22). In today's unisex society, it is easy to forget we are different and we're supposed to be different from a man. Paul gave an excellent example in 1 Timothy 4:12 of how to be a good Christian when he said not to let people treat you unimportant just because you are young. Rather, you have an excellent opportunity while you are young to be an example to others of a fine, young Christian woman by your speech, actions, love, faith, and pure life.

- *Never Give Up on God.* "For He Himself has said, 'I will never leave you nor forsake you. So we may boldly say: 'The Lord is my helper; I will not fear. What can man do to me?' " (Hebrews 13:5–6). Sometimes it can be frightening to face new challenges and situations. Those times are not as frightening when you have the assurance that God will never leave you. Regardless of how insignificant it may be, God is God, and He knows what is going on in your life, and He cares. Throughout your life, you may be faced with difficult people, challenging jobs, disabled or difficult children, sicknesses, or any number of things, but as a Christian, you must never give up on God. You have the promise that He will truly never forsake you.

- *If You're Going to Be a Christian—Be a Christian!* "And do not be conformed to this world, but be transformed by the renewing of your mind, that you may prove what is that good and acceptable and perfect will of God" (Romans 12:2). Don't be molded into the world's pattern. Take a stand for something or you'll fall for anything and everything. Let your light shine before others so they can see Christ living in you. People see through insincerity and can easily spot a fake. Christianity is the best life. Give it all you can. Be the real thing—be a Christian.

Living a Life of Love

Our world was thrown into turmoil immediately following the devastating terrorist attacks on the United States at the Pentagon and the World Trade Center. After the initial reactions of shock, disbelief, and anger, we rallied in love and support for our country and turned to God more than in times past. With our future uncertain, we are still reaching out more than ever before in love for one another.

In contrast to these acts of hatred, Jesus' greatest message was that of love. He taught that the greatest commandment was to love God with all our hearts, soul, and mind, and the second was to love our neighbors as ourselves. Jesus told us to love our enemies. He said all men would know that we were His disciples by our love for one another.

Love will motivate us to obey His commandments and cause us to live better lives. It's one of the most important qualities we can possess. We must show our love to others, teach others the truth in love, and love our enemies. Paul said in the Bible's beautiful love chapter:

> Though I speak with the tongues of men and of angels, but have not love, I have become sounding brass or a clanging symbol . . . And though I bestow all my goods to feed the poor, and though I give my body to be burned, but have not love, it profits me nothing (1 Corinthians 13:1–3).

Love is the greatest motivator and the foundation for Christianity. God's love for all mankind in sending His Son to die for our sins was the ultimate sacrifice and expression of love.

The Christian life God gives us through that love is the only life that makes sense. It's the best life. A compromising Christian will never be happy straddling the fence—trying to hold on to the world and Christianity at the same time. It doesn't work, and God won't accept it anyway. He has promised in Revelation 3:16 to spew from His mouth those Christians who are lukewarm toward Him, being neither hot nor cold.

If you find yourself straddling the fence or if you have led a life of compromise, I urge you as a young Christian woman to have the character, conviction, and courage to get off the fence and stay off. Take a stand for Christ and be counted on to do what is right by leaning on the Lord to guide you in making all your decisions.

As a young Christian woman, go for the best—for now and for eternity. You deserve the best. It can indeed be a wonderful life!

1. Are there different degrees of sinning or is one sin any worse than another? Support your answer.

2. What does the Bible teach about the nature of specific sins? For example, is the sin of greed or gossip as bad as that of homosexuality, adultery or murder? Why or why not?

3. Why is it so hard for people to forgive themselves?

4. Name a sin that God will not forgive.

5. What does it mean to straddle the fence? Is it always bad to straddle the fence?

6. What are some ways you can avoid being a fence straddler?

7. What are some ways in which you can make good choices?

8. How can guilt be used in a positive way?

9. What is apathy and why is it so dangerous for a Christian?

10. What are some ways in which you can live a balanced life?

Bibliography

Books

Barton, Dr. Bruce B., ed. *Life Application Bible Commentary,* 98, 494, 1674, 1997, 2071, 2139. Wheaton, IL and Grand Rapids, MI: Tyndale House Publishers and Zondervan Publishing House, 1991.

Blitchington, W. Peter. *The Christian Woman's Search for Self-Esteem,* 41, 46, 82, 107. Nashville: Thomas Nelson Publishers, 1982.

Choate, Betty Burton, *The Role of Woman.* Winona, MS: J. C. Choate Publications, 1999.

Davis, John Jefferson. *Abortion and the Christian: What Every Believer Should Know,* 27–28, 125. Phillipsburg: NJ: Presbyterian and Reformed Publishing Company, 1984.

Duke, Kerry. *God at a Distance.* 88–89. Huntsville, AL: Publishing Designs, Inc., 1995.

Dobson, James. *Life on the Edge,* 49–50, 207, 209, 236, 243–244. Dallas: Word Publishing, 1995.

Eichman, Nancy. *Seasoning Your Words: God's Recipe for Controlling Your Tongue,* 74. Nashville: Gospel Advocate Company, 1997.

Hewlett, Sylvia Ann. *Creating a Life: Professional Women and the Quest for Children.* Talk Miramax, 2002.

Jenkins, Jerry. *Twelve Things I Want My Kids to Remember Forever,* 127–128. Chicago: Moody Press, 1991.

Johnston, Joni. *Appearance Obsession: Learning to Love the Way You Look,* 23, 98–99, 141, 163, 174, 179, 202–205. Deerfield Beach, FL: Health Communications, Inc., 1994.

Judges, Daniel P. *Hard Choices, Lost Voices: How the Abortion Conflict Has Divided America, Distorted Constitutional Rights, and Damaged the Courts,* 58, 66–68, 114. Chicago, IL: Ivan R. Dee, 1993.

Kesler, Jay. *Ten Mistakes Parents Make With Teenagers (And How to Avoid Them)*, 48–49, 76. Brentwood, TN: Wolgemuth and Hyatt Publishers, Inc., 1998.

Mahkorn, Sandra. *Pregnancy and Sexual Assault: The Psychological Aspects of Abortion*, 55–69. Washington, D. C.: University Publications of America, 1979.

Mains, Karen Burton. *You Are What You Say*. Grand Rapids, MI: Zondervan Publishing House, 1988.

McArthur, John. *Whose Money Is It Anyway?* Nashville: Word Publishing, 2000.

McWhorter, Don. *God's Woman: Feminine or Feminist?* Huntsville, AL: Publishing Designs, Inc., 1992.

McWhorter, Jane. *Now I Can Fly!* 68–69. Abilene, TX: Quality Publications, 1985.

Meisler, Andy, and Norma McCorvey. *I Am Roe: My Life, Roe v. Wade, and Freedom of Choices*, 7. New York, NY: Harper Collins Publishers, 1994.

Mueller, Walt. *Understanding Today's Youth Culture*, 126, 139–140, 213–218, 230, 264. Wheaten, IL: Tyndale House, 1994.

Maynard, R. A., ed. *Kids Having Kids: A Robin Hood Foundation Special Report*. New York: Robin Hood Foundation, 1996.

Paul, Pamela. *The Starter Marriage and the Future of Marriage*, 2002.

Schmidt, Thomas E. *Straight and Narrow? Compassion and Clarity in the Homosexual Debate*, 26–27, 102–103, 106. Louisville, KY: Westminister John Knox Press, 1995.

Senter, Ruth. *Have We Really Come a Long Way?* 25. Minneapolis, MN: Bethany House Publishers, 1997.

Shelly, Rubel. *Young People and Their Lord*, 173. Nashville, TN: Twentieth Century Christian, 1987.

Skoglund, Elizabeth. *You Can Be Your Own Child's Counselor*, 21–22. Glendale, CA: Regal Books, 1978.

Simmons, Randy. *Straight Talk for Teens*, 26–27. Nashville, TN: Christian Communications, 1987.

Smith, E. Leon. *Stewardship and Spiritual Maturity*. Ft. Worth, TX: Star Bible Publications, 1995.

Smith, F. LaGard. *What Most Women Want: What Few Women Find*. Eugene, OR: Harvest House Publishers, 1992.

Soards, Marion L. *Scripture and Homosexuality, Biblical Authority and the Church Today*. Louisville, KY: Westminister John Knox Press, 1995.

Stafford, Tim. *Sexual Chaos*, 134–135. Dowers Grove, IL: InterVarsity Press, 1989.

Young, Ben, and Samuel Adams. *The Ten Commandments of Dating*, 54, 87, 89. Nashville, TN: Nelson Publisher, 1999.

Church Bulletin

Wacaster, Tom, Jr. "Sitting on the Fence." The Lincoln Light 36 (2002).

Fact Sheets

Alcohol Advisory Council Fact Sheet, 1999.

America's Health Network, September 1996.

Mothers Against Drunk Driving (MADD) Fact Sheet, 2000.

The Christian Connection, Pornography Fact Sheet, February 1994, 19.

U.S. Drug Enforcement Administration (DEA) Drug Facts.

Internet Articles

"A Tribute to Mothers," 1999.

DanceSafe Organization. "What is Ecstasy?" April 2000. Website: http://www.dancesafe.org

"Date Rape Drugs," *Rape Crisis Assistance and Prevention (RCAP),* "Date Rape Drugs," Website: http://www.watervillerape.org

Maryland Underage Drinking Prevention Coalition (MUDPC), webmaster@mudpc.org 2000.

Meserve, Jeanne. "Promise Keepers: Supporting or Oppressing Women?" October 4, 1997.

Mothers Against Drunk Driving (MADD) Fact Sheet, 2000.

North Dakota Division of Alcohol and Drugs. "Alcohol and Women," 1999.

"On Being a Mother." 1999.

Promise Keepers . . . CNN Interactive News, Jeanne Mexerve.

Resnick, Meredith. "The Bureau for At-Risk Youth: Teen Talk," 1999. Website: http://www.at-risk.com

Magazines and Newspapers

Anderson, Brian C. "An 'A' for Home Schooling." *City Journal,* Vol. 10, No. 3, Summer 2000.

Bayder, Nazli, *Homemade,* 1998.

"Breakpoint with Charles Colson," Vol. 1, No. 6, August 1991.

Cantrell, Robbie. (Unpublished), "If You Want to be Happy for the Rest of Your Life." *Modesty and Marriage Lessons,* September 2000.

Chulindra, Waria. "Living Together Before Marriage Becoming More Common." *Knight Rider News Service,* Beverly LaHaye Institute statistics, 1999, September 25, 2000.

France, David, and Debra Rosenburg. "The Abortion Pill." *Newsweek Magazine,* October 9, 2000, 28–29.

Good Housekeeping Magazine, September 2000, 70.

Hafften, Ann. "Feinist Generation Gap Emerges at Re-Imagining Conference." *Religion News Service,* November 11, 2000.

Holland, Tom. "Works of the Flesh: Homosexuality." Gospel tract, undated.

Jerome, Richard. "A Body to Die For." *People Magazine,* October 30, 2000, 109.

Josphson, Joseph and Edna. *Institute of Ethics,* 2000.

Kin, Walter. "Should You Stay Together for the Kids?" *Time Magazine,* September 25, 2000, 75–82.

Meerve, Jeanne. "Promise Keepers: Supporting or Oppressing Women?" October 4, 1997.

Peterson, Karen. "Having It All—Except Children." *USA Today,* April 8, 2002.

———. "Homosexuality No Longer Fazes Most Teens." *USA Today*, February 29, 2000.

———. "Starter Marriage: A New Term for Early Divorce." *USA Today,* January 29, 2001.

Rubin, Sabrina. "Binge Drinking: A Campus Killer." *Reader's Digest.* Pleasantville NY: Bernadette Harrison Haley Publisher, Vol. 153, No. 919, November 1998, 75–81.

Taylor, Irene C. "The Women's Movement Then and Now." *The Firm Foundation.* October 1992.

Thames, Beth. *The Huntsville Times.* "Girls Who Dress Like Grown-ups Get Attention in All the Wrong Ways," October 7, 2000, E-1.

Wallerstein, Judith, Julia Lewis, and Sandra Blakeslee. "Fear of Falling." *Time Magazine,* September 25, 2000, 85–88.

Webster, Allen. "Wait Till the Honeymoon?" *House to House / Heart to Heart.* Gospel tract, undated.

Newspapers Articles (Unknown Authors)

"Profanity Used Every Six Minutes on TV." *Chicago Sun-Times,* December 20, 1999.

"Snapshot: Average Age to Tie the Knot." *USA Today,* May 9, 2000.

"What They Didn't Tell Me About Abortion." *Today's Christian Woman,* Sep/Oct 1996.

"What Does the Bible Say About Lying?" Copticenter, Inc., 1999.

"What is Title IX—and Why do I Care?" The Feminist Majority Foundation and New Media Publishing, Inc., 1995.

Public Documents

National Clearinghouse for Alcohol and Drug Information (NCADI), Healthtouch Online, www.healthtouch.com, 1995–2000.

National Highway Traffic Safety Administration (NHTSA), 1998 Statistics.

National Institute on Drug Abuse. "U. S. Senate Caucus on International Narcotics Control," July 25, 2000.

National Women's Health Information Center, U. S. Department of Health and Human Services. "Date Rape Drugs (Rohypnol)," December 1, 2000.

North Dakota Division of Alcohol and Drugs. "Alcohol and Women," 1999.

Texas Commission on Alcohol and Drug Abuse. "Rohypnol and GHB: Just the Facts," September 25, 1998.

U.S. Bureau of Census Current Population Report, Series P-60, Women's Bureau, February 2000.

U.S. Department of Labor Women's Bureau. "20 Facts on Women Working," March 2000.

Youth Intelligence Marketing Firm, 1990.

Note

Special thanks and credit for much of the theological discussion contained in chapter 11 regarding the role of women in the church must be given to Don McWhorter, *God's Woman: Feminine or Feminist?;* F. LaGard Smith, *What Most Women Want: What Few Women Find;* and Betty Burton Choate, *Role of Woman.*